P9-CIW-957

the complete book of

WREATHS

WITHDRAWN

the complete book of
WREATHS

200
delightful
& creative
designs

Chris Rankin

CONTRIBUTING WRITERS:
Carol Taylor
Rob Pulleyn
Deborah Morgenthal
Leslie Dierks
Dawn Cusick
Eric Carlson

LARK BOOKS

A Division of Sterling Publishing Co., Inc.

New York

Book and Cover Designer: *Theresa Gwynn*

Photographers: *Evan Bracken, Martin Fox*

Editorial Assistants: *Catharine Sutherland, Heather Smith, Emma Jones, Veronika Alice Gunter*

Production Assistant: *M.E. Kirby*

Library of Congress Cataloging-in-Publication Data

Rankin, Chris
  The complete book of wreaths : 200 delightful & creative designs / Chris Rankin;
  contributing writers, Carol Taylor ... [et al.].
    p. cm.
   ISBN 1-57990-208-1 (paper)
   1. Wreaths. I. Title.

TT899.75 .R36 2001
745.92'6—dc21

00-052910

10 9 8 7 6 5 4 3 2 1

Published by Lark Books, a division of
Sterling Publishing Co., Inc.
387 Park Avenue South, New York, N.Y. 10016

Material in this book was adapted from The Wreath Book (© 1988), Wreaths 'Round the Year (© 1990), A Scented Christmas (© 1990), Christmas Naturals (© 1991), The Holiday Wreath Book (© 1992), Herbal Wreaths (© 1992), Wreath Making Basics (© 1993), Wreath Magic (© 1994), Wreaths Around the House (© 1994), Wreaths from the Garden (© 1995), and Dried Flower Crafts (© 1995).

© 2001, Lark Books

Distributed in Canada by Sterling Publishing, c/o Canadian Manda Group,
  One Atlantic Ave., Suite 105, Toronto, Ontario, Canada M6K 3E7

Distributed in Australia by Capricorn Link (Australia) Pty Ltd., P.O. Box 6651,
  Baulkham Hills, Business Centre, NSW 2153, Australia

Distributed in the U.K. by Guild of Master Craftsman Publications Ltd.,
  Castle Place, 166 High Street, Lewes, East Sussex, England BN7 1XU
  Tel: (+ 44) 1273 477374, Fax: (+ 44) 1273 478606, Email: pubs@thegmcgroup.com,
  Web: www.gmcpublications.com

The written instructions, photographs, designs, patterns, and projects in this volume are intended for the personal use of the reader and may be reproduced for that purpose only. Any other use, especially commercial use, is forbidden under law without written permission of the copyright holder.

Every effort has been made to ensure that all the information in this book is accurate. However, due to differing conditions, tools, and individual skills, the publisher cannot be responsible for any injuries, losses, and other damages that may result from the use of the information in this book.

If you have questions or comments about this book, please contact:
Lark Books
50 College St.
Asheville, NC 28801
(828) 253-0467

Printed in China
All rights reserved

ISBN 1-57990-208-1

Dedicated to

Fred Tyson Gaylor,

an incredible designer and

an incredible person

Table of Contents

Introduction

Almost all of us can conjure up images of wreaths from the potpourri of our childhood memories. At the very least, we remember the festive holiday wreaths that adorned front doors during the Christmas season, with fragrant evergreen boughs, crisp pinecones, and bright red bows.

The use of wreaths to celebrate and decorate goes back much further than our own childhoods. In ancient Persian and Greek cultures, wreaths were called diadems, from the Greek word *diadema*, meaning "a thing bound around." A diadem was a band of fabric worn around the brow of a royal bonnet, symbolizing royalty.

Wreaths made of various leaves were also used as prizes during the Greek Olympics. Each host city would award head garlands made of local trees, such as olive and laurel. Thus originated the olive leaf as a peace symbol and the phrase, "to earn your laurels."

To the Romans, the Greek royal headdresses were seen as symbols of royalty, and thus despotic power. They were an insult to their high regard for democracy and were fervently shunned. However, the Roman upper classes adopted the headdresses as an item of fashion and wore garlands of oak leaves and laurel. These head wreaths also became symbols of military and athletic prowess, and were worn with great pride. When Julius Caesar became leader, the Romans promptly crowned their victorious general with a wreath of fresh laurel.

Diadems and head wreaths did not go unnoticed by the rest of the world's elite, and soon the upper classes of other countries were designing headdresses of their own. Precious jewels and metals were added, eventually creating the ornate crowns we have come to associate with royalty. In fact, the word crown derives from the Latin word corona, meaning garland or wreath. The concept of a crown as a symbol for royalty was firmly seated in tradition by the 15th century. In time, all social classes took to wearing wreaths to celebrate special occasions and to honor religious holidays.

Plants were a natural choice for wreath ingredients. Most ancient cultures worshipped trees a symbols of divine energy, and arrangements of boughs and sprigs embodied both secular and religious meaning. Holly, mistletoe, and other evergreens, for example, were brought indoors during the cold of winter as a symbolic offering of shelter to the sylvan spirits. A woman who accepted the advances of a lover gave him a crown of birch; if rejected, he received a crown of hazel. Because the circle symbolizes eternity, the wreath also became a natural and fitting addition to funerals.

Exactly when the transition from "wreath as head ornament" to "wreath as wall decoration" occurred is unclear, but it seems quite possible that someone enamored with a festival headdress hung it on a wall instead of throwing it away.

The process of putting this book together has been fascinating—from learning the history of wreaths to discovering how wreaths are currently used. No longer do we see wreaths limited to the front door or over the fireplace. A beautiful deep-toned wreath of dried flowers or herbs is as appropriate in a formal living room as a Christmas wreath is on the front door. Holiday season wreaths of evergreen and pinecones are still popular, and in fact we devote many pages to this tradition, but we also wanted to share with you the rich variety of wreath styles and designs being made today.

An interesting aspect of contemporary wreaths is function. While those of the classical past were essentially symbolic in nature and those of the Victorian era were purely decorative, many of the wreaths in this book actually serve a practical purpose. You will find wreaths made into napkin holders, air fragrancers, and spice racks. You will also discover edible wreaths, jewelry, and display cases for treasured collectibles.

Another exciting discovery is how a wreath reflects the creative style and personality of its maker. The wreath designers who contributed to this book are diverse—they are nurserymen, floral designers, and even the author's children. However, they all have one very important thing in common: a love for their materials and a heartfelt joy in making wreaths.

When you begin making your own wreaths you will be amazed to discover yet another design style—your own. Even when you try to duplicate one of the designs in this book, you will undoubtedly make subtle changes, adding different ingredients, or rearranging their order. Enjoy your personalized interpretation of these wreath designs and be assured that it's difficult to make an unattractive wreath. If you're not delighted by the results of a particular project, simply add a few new ingredients to perk it up or take the wreath apart and start over again. Above all, have fun!

—Chris Rankin

Wreath Making Basics

WREATHMAKING MAY well be one of the simplest, most pleasurable crafts you will ever undertake. You can replicate a wreath from this book down to the most minute detail, or you can make small (or large) changes to suit the materials on hand and your own personal style. The pages that follow review a variety of techniques that will help you to make great wreaths. None of them is difficult to master, and there are no hard and fast rules to remember. If you don't happen to have floral picks on hand, you can easily attach stems of blooms with thin-gauge wire or monofilament. If you don't like using a glue gun, just attach the item with ribbon. There are no wreath police—just have fun.

BASES

*T*HERE'S NO GETTING AROUND IT—EVERY wreath must begin with a base. The type, style, size, shape, and cost of your wreath's base, though, is completely up to you. The straw, moss, and vine bases favored by traditional wreath makers are still available, but so are a range of creative options such as foam bases with mirrored centers, bases covered with grated cinnamon, bases made with wet foam to lengthen the life span of fresh flowers, and much, much more. This wide variety of base materials (with corresponding varieties in sizes, price ranges, and technical considerations) makes it a good idea to have a visual idea of the type of wreath you'd like to make before you choose a base. The pages that follow explain many of the benefits, drawbacks, attachment methods, and design strengths relevant to each type of base.

FOAM BASES

Foam bases are comparatively inexpensive and available in more varieties of thickness, size, and shape than any other type of wreath base. You can find them as small as 2 inches (5 cm) in diameter, in narrow heart shapes, and even large ovals. The biggest drawback to foam bases is they can really distract from the beauty of a finished wreath if small holes or gaps are visible. Many wreath makers dislike the foam surface for glue adhesion: some craft glues just peel off while some hot glues are hot enough to melt the foam. These two problems, though, can be easily solved by covering the foam surface before you begin working.

The two most popular materials to cover foam bases are moss and ribbon. Spanish, sheet, and other varieties of moss can be folded around the base and secured in place as needed with floral pins. The smaller your wreath base, though, the more difficulty you'll have using the floral pins. Ribbon sometimes makes a better choice because you can match the ribbon's color to the wreath's materials. With very small bases, choose a narrower ribbon and secure it to the foam with sewing pins. If portions of the base will not show in the finished base, you can substitute strips of cotton fabric for the ribbon.

Many of the larger foam bases are available with a thick wire ring that's been molded with the foam to add strength when you're working with heavy materials. Wire-reinforced foam bases should also be used when the materials will not be evenly arranged around the base to prevent the stress of unequal weight distribution from cracking the foam.

WIRE BASES

Single-wire bases are the ideal choice when working with lightweight materials such as pussy willow, pepperberries, and dried flowers because the finished wreath will be thin and delicate, creating a pleasant design reiteration of the materials. Be sure you consider where you'll be displaying this type of wreath before making it. The wreath will look wonderful in a small room, centered over a light piece of furniture, but will look out of place in a very large room or centered over a large focal point such as a rock fireplace. Single-wire wreath bases are not a good choice when you're working with larger items because there just isn't enough surface area to glue things onto, and it's impossible to arrange the materials at interesting angles without creating lots of unattractive gaps. Single-wire wreath bases will not accommodate a lot of weight.

Double-wire wreath bases are also available, allowing you to create a flat, wide surface by wrapping brown shipping paper or a colorful paper ribbon around the two wire rings. This kind of base creates less of a

three-dimensional wreath, so this is a good base choice if you're making a wreath to display in the narrow space between a storm door and an outside door. The flat surface created by covering the rings with paper also enables you to work with large, delicate materials such as dried peppers that would break if you tried to fold them around the curves of a foam, straw, or vine base. Like single-wire bases, this type of base cannot support heavy items. If you anticipate not having enough materials to densely cover the base, be sure to choose the paper or ribbon in a color compatible with the materials so the spaces won't be too obvious in the finished wreath.

Wire wreath bases are also available with multiple rings of wire that have been arranged at different depths, forming a trench that can be filled with moss, pine needles, or fragrant herbs such as sweet Annie or mint. These custom bases are ideal if you have only a few dried flowers to work with but you want a round, full-shaped wreath. If you plan to display the wreath on a table, just arrange the materials compactly inside the trench, taking care to conceal the outer wire ring; if the finished wreath will be hung on a wall, you will need to secure the materials inside the trench by loosely wrapping monofilament or thin-gauge floral wire around the materials and the base. Single leaves or flower blooms can then be hot-glued directly on top of the base or dabbed with craft glue and inserted into the base material.

because the straw is so thick that the center hole begins to fill in as the diameter of the base decreases.

To prevent the stems of dried flowers and herbs from breaking when they're inserted into a straw base, materials are usually first attached to floral picks, and the picks are then inserted into the base. Contemporary wreath designers, however, have increased the versatility of straw bases by leaving portions of the straw showing in the finished wreath and by wrapping the straw with paper ribbon to create a surface more receptive to hot glue. The straw bases available in craft stores are often covered with a thin layer of green plastic. If straw tends to make you sneeze, you can leave the plastic on and just insert the picks right through the plastic. You can also make your own straw bases with the instructions on page 17.

VINE BASES

Vine bases are an all-around good choice for a multitude of reasons. The natural vine is so attractive that designers often leave large portions of the base uncovered, so you need far fewer materials to make a vine wreath. Vine bases also accommodate a wide range of styles. With simple everlastings and a polka dot bow, the wreath looks country; add some dried fruit, some exotic flowers, and the wreath will work in even the most formal of homes. When shopping for vine bases, look for firm, nicely colored vine with a multitude of curly tendrils.

Vine bases are also easy to make if you have access to vine (see page 18). Wreaths displayed over large walls or fireplaces are often made from vine bases because even a 6-foot-diameter (1.8 m) vine base is fairly lightweight. If you're custom-making a vine base for a

STRAW BASES

Straw wreath bases have long been the first choice among traditional wreath makers, perhaps because it's difficult to top the lush fullness of a straw base that's been decorated with dried flowers. Not everyone has access to enough dried flowers to cover the full surface area of a straw base, though, and buying the dried flowers in bulk from a craft store can get pricey. Straw bases also do not come in the same variety of sizes as other bases

specific location, check to be sure the base is proportionate to the display location and add more rows of vine to increase the size if necessary.

To attach materials to a vine base, hot-gluing and wiring are the methods of choice. If you're working with multiple stems of dried flowers or herbs, they can be attached to a floral pick (see page 19) and then inserted at an angle into the vines after a dab of hot glue has been added to the end of the pick. Fresh and silk fruits and vegetables, which seem to go so well with vine bases, can be wired (see pages 22 and 23) to the base and then reinforced with a dab of hot glue if necessary. Before you actually attach your materials to the base, though, be sure to hold them against the vines to see if you like the effect—dark-colored materials sometimes blend in too much to be appreciated, whereas bright-colored materials contrast very well.

MOSS BASES

Moss bases are well-liked for several reasons. First, they provide a good adhesion surface for glue as well as being receptive to floral picks and single stems of flowers or greenery. Second, their natural look allows wreath makers to decorate the top, bottom, or just one side of the base and leave the remaining surface area bare for an attractive alternative to the traditional-looking wreath. You can purchase several sizes of moss bases in craft supply stores or make them your-self from scratch. (See pages 16 and 17 for directions.) You can also cover a foam or straw base with moss to create a surface that's more receptive to hot glue. To cover a straw base with moss, just arrange the moss around the top and sides, and then secure in place with floral pins or with loose wraps of monofilament or thin-gauge floral wire.

Several varieties of mosses are sold in small packages in craft stores. If you opt to pick your own moss, however, be sure to find out which varieties, if any, are endangered in your area. Even if your choice isn't endangered, it's still a good idea to harvest only a little moss from each area so you don't damage the ecosystem.

HERB BASES

'Silver King' and 'Silver Queen' artemisias make a wonderful base material for wreaths. The feathery, silver foliage of this perennial herb makes it an ideal background for dried flower and herb wreaths. Pastels seem to blend right in to the delicate gray of the artemisia, while bright colors seem brighter with the contrast. The fresh, clean scent is a nice bonus.

You can order these artemisias in dried bunches from herb farms or grow them yourself. Like most herbs, the plants don't mind dry soil and hot sun, and they re-seed themselves, so if you buy one plant this year you may well have ten plants next year.

To make dried artemisia into a wreath base, hold it against a single-wire ring or place it in a trench wire base

you like by simply rolling a few of the seeds be-tween your fingers. The delicate look of the small blooms and foliage makes this the perfect back-ground material for dried flowers in pastel colors, such as pink larkspur, miniature carnations, and miniature roses.

To make dried sweet Annie into a wreath base, hold several dried stems against a single-wire ring or place it in a trench wire base and secure by wrapping several times with monofilament or thin-gauge floral wire. Single dried flower blooms can then be hot-glued into the sweet Annie, while the stems of dried flowers and foliage can be dabbed with hot glue and inserted deep into the sweet Annie.

Fragrant culinary herbs make the perfect base for kitchen wreaths. If you're new to growing herbs, you may find the idea of making wreath bases from fresh-cut plants just scandalous. With most perennial herbs, though, you'll have lots of extra plants to spare after the first year of growth, and by the third year you'll be making culinary wreaths for everyone on your gift list.

Bay, oregano, and sage make lovely backgrounds for whole heads of garlic or dried red peppers. If you live in a climate that's warm year 'round, you can trim a bay tree for leaves. If you live in an area where bay isn't

and secure by wrapping several times with monofila-ment or thin-gauge floral wire. Single dried flower blooms can then be hot-glued onto the artemisia, while stems of dried flowers and foliage can be dabbed with hot glue and inserted deep into the artemisia.

Sweet Annie, actually a type of artemisia, has been cultivated for its fragrance for centuries. A hardy perennial, sweet Annie likes sun and doesn't mind dry soil, so you may wish to grow it yourself rather than purchase it from an herb farm or craft supply store. Harvest the plant any time after it has bloomed, and hang it upside down to dry in bunches of four to six stems.

Few people find Sweet Annie's pun-gent yet clean fragrance objectionable, and the fragrance can be released whenever

winter-hardy (and thus is more difficult and expensive to come by), you can order a pre-made bay base from an herb farm.

Wreath makers value bee balm for its beautiful, fragrant blooms ranging in color from pastel pink and lavender to a brilliant magenta. Like other members of the mint family, this innocent-looking perennial throws root runners and multiplies with great speed.

While you may be familiar only with peppermint or spearmint, there's a whole world of mints out there just waiting to be discovered by wreath makers. Ginger mint, orange mint, grapefruit mint, pineapple mint, apple mint, and chocolate mint are just a few. The foliage usually dries to a nice dark green, and the fragrances remain subtle for years.

To make dried bay or sage leaves into a wreath base, attach 3-inch (7.5 cm) stems of bay to floral picks (see page 19) and insert the picks into a straw base. For a thinner base, hold the stems against a single-wire ring and secure them by wrapping several times with floral wire. Continue positioning additional stems to overlap the stems of the previous leaves until the entire wire ring is covered.

To make dried oregano, bee balm, or mint into a wreath base, hold several stems against a single-wire ring or place it in a trench wire base and secure with several wraps of monofilament or thin-gauge floral wire. Single herb blooms and/or culinary items can then be hot-glued onto the oregano, while stems of dried herbs and foliage can be dabbed with hot-glue and inserted deep into the oregano.

INNOVATIVE BASES

$\mathcal{S}$URPRISINGLY ENOUGH, WREATH BASES CAN be crafted into gardens for many living plants. A few garden shops and mail-order houses carry these types of bases pre-made, but you can make your own at home with not too much effort. To make the base you will need fine chicken wire, a heavy-duty stapler, moss, potting soil, wire cutters, plywood, and several cooperative plants. First, trace the circle shape of a large straw or vine wreath base onto a piece of ply-

wood and cut out the doughnut center and the outer edges. Then mold the chicken wire over the top of the wood base and staple it to the back side. Soak the moss in water and then pack it with equal amounts of potting soil into the chicken wire. Last, plant an assortment of succulents (or other easily-rooted plant) around the wreath. To increase visual appeal, small mushrooms and fungi can be hot-glued to the moss. Keep the wreath sitting flat for a few weeks so the plants can take root. The wreath can be hung indoors, although you may want to take it down when you water it every few days.

A simple foam base covered with cinnamon emits a rich fragrance even after it's been decorated, and the fragrance can be rejuvenated as needed with a few drops of cinnamon-scented essential oil. Materials can be picked, wired, or hot-glued to the cinnamon base just as you would any other foam base, but it makes sense to choose a design that leaves a portion of the base showing, as the wreath shown above does. Although you could make an afternoon project of crushing cinnamon sticks and gluing the powder to a foam base, it's a lot easier to purchase the wreath pre-covered and spend your energy making the wreath instead.

A very simple idea—mounting a piece of glass against the back of a foam base—creates a base with potential for creating very elegant, formal wreaths that make ideal decorations for wedding and anniversary celebrations. You can attach the mirror to the back of a base yourself with hot glue, or purchase the base pre-assembled from most larger craft stores. Materials are inserted into or hot-glued to the foam base just as you would any other foam base. The reflections add an intriguing multi-dimensional appeal, which can be increased by using brightly colored materials. These wreaths make the perfect decorations for celebration parties.

piece of foam, and then cutting out the shape with a serrated knife. The foam was then sculpted with the knife to create various levels, and then decorated by hot-gluing individual flowers and leaves in place.

Unique wreath shapes can also be made by securing several purchased wire or foam bases together with duct tape or heavy-gauge floral wire, or by unfolding coat hangers and reshaping them in interlocking

WREATH SHAPES

*W*REATHS ARE WELL KNOWN FOR THEIR round shape, which was probably originally chosen for its symbolic meanings of fullness, completeness, and coming together. But perhaps because the circle shape is so entrenched in history, making wreaths with other shapes is downright exciting, a chance to throw caution to the wind and break tradition, even for the most conservative of us.

The bases for shapes such as ovals and hearts can be purchased in craft supply stores, while others will need to be made at home with some imagination and a cooperative material such as fresh-cut vine, foam, or floral wire.

The base for the unusual wreath shown at right was made by drawing the pattern on a piece of paper, gluing the paper to a

positions. If you undertake this type of wreaths, though, you'll need to add extra details to make them look right as a whole. Try tying the look together with streamers from a French ribbon bow or adding extra flower accents in a strategic location.

HANDMADE BASES

*T*O MAKE A STRAW BASE YOU WILL NEED several handfuls of straw, an unfolded coat hanger or length of heavy-gauge wire, and a spool of thin-gauge floral wire or monofilament.

First, shape the coat hanger or heavy-gauge wire into a circle that's at least 12 inches (30 cm) in diameter. Next, gather a small handful of straw and position it against the wire ring. Secure the straw to the wire circle by wrapping the wire or monofilament several times around the straw and the wire circle in 1½- to 2-inch (4 to 5 cm) intervals.

Continue adding new handfuls of straw to the wire circle as described above until the entire base is covered. Wrap the wire around the straw several times in the same place and trim it with wire cutters. The straw base can now be shaped into a better looking circle if desired.

To make a vine wreath base you will need six to eight lengths of fresh-cut vine. If fresh-cut vines are not available, you can soak older vines in a tub of warm water until they soften, which may take several hours or several days. When choosing vines, look for firm, well-shaped lengths with lots of tendrils and no weak spots from insect damage.

After you've chosen your vines, curve four to six of them around to form a circle, allowing an overlap of about 2 inches (5 cm). Then wrap one or two longer vines around the circle to hold the first vines in place.

Moss bases can be made in several ways. To make a moss base from scratch, you will need several large handfuls of Spanish moss, an unfolded coat hanger or length of heavy-gauge wire, and a spool of medium-gauge wire or monofilament. First, shape the coat hanger or heavy-gauge wire into a circle. Next, hold a large handful of moss against the wire circle and secure the moss in place by wrapping several times with the spool wire or monofilament in 1½- to 2-inch (4 to 5 cm)

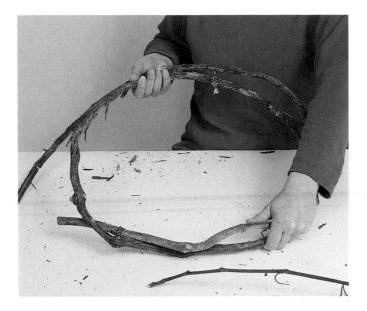

intervals. Continue adding handfuls of moss to the wire circle until the entire base is formed. If you're happy with the thickness of your base, you can stop here; or you can increase the surface area of the wreath base by adding more layers of moss.

Moss bases can also be created with a couple of large handfuls of moss, a straw or foam base, and several floral pins. Just curve the moss around the base and secure in place as needed with floral pins. Fresh-picked mosses should be secured in place while they're still damp to prevent breakage.

TOOLS & NIFTY GADGETS

A GREAT COLLECTION OF HELPFUL TOOLS awaits you at your local craft store. They're all easy to use, inexpensive, and will save you lots of time.

FLORAL PICKS

These wonderful gadgets are actually small wooden picks with short lengths of fine-gauge wire attached. They are used to secure stems of flowers or foliage that are too weak to insert directly into a foam or straw base. The end of the pick is pre-cut at an angle to make perforation into the base easier. Floral picks can also be used as a time-saving device: Instead of picking one stem into a base at a time, you can attach

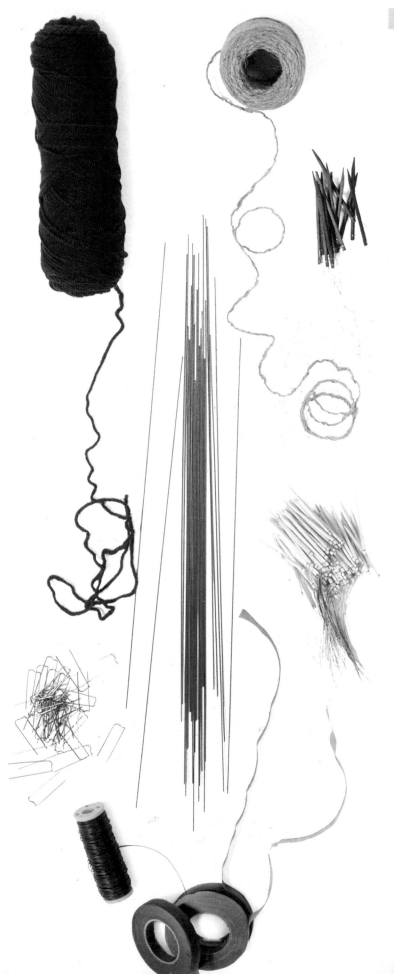

small bouquets of materials to a single pick. There's no set rule about how many stems should be in each bouquet. Three to five is a good guideline, but some materials may have such thin stems that you can pick eight or nine together, while others may be so thick that you'll have difficulty attaching two stems to a floral pick.

To use a floral pick, position the pick against the stem(s) so the pick extends about 1 inch (2.5 cm) below the stems. Wrap the wire around the stems twice in the same place, then wrap and spiral the wire down around the stems and the pick to bind them together. Trim the stems where the wire ends. If the stems are especially fragile, you can add strength by wrapping the picked stems with floral tape.

Floral picks work best with compact straw bases. They will also work with foam bases if the foam is very dense and you don't insert the picks too close together. Floral picks can be used with vine bases if the vines are woven closely together; if the vine weave is loose, you may need to add a dab of hot glue to the tip of each pick before inserting it into the vine.

CRAFT PICKS

Craft picks are floral picks without the wire, and they're used primarily to attach materials such as fresh fruits and vegetables to a craft base. The sharp end of the pick easily perforates the fruit or vegetable, and then the protruding end is hot-glued into a foam, straw, or vine base.

FLORAL PINS

These U-shaped pieces of wire look and work like old-fashioned hairpins. Purchase the pins in a color (green and silver are available) that will blend in with your materials. To use a floral pin, simply position the materials you're attaching against a straw, foam, or moss base, position the pin with its prongs on either side of the material, and press the pin into the base at an angle.

FLORAL TAPE

Floral tape comes in several shades of brown and green that are compatible with natural materials. Floral tape is most often used to add strength to a floral pick that's holding multiple delicate stems. The only trick to

success with floral tape is to stretch it gently as you're working with it to increase its adhesive quality.

GLUE GUNS

Although you could make lots of very nice wreaths without ever using a glue gun, you will miss out on a lot of creative fun if you try to work without one. Glue guns enable you to attach virtually anything to a wreath base in just seconds. So if you're spread out on your kitchen table this winter making a Christmas wreath and you run out of (or get tired of) holly berries, your glue gun enables you to send a roving eye around the house for

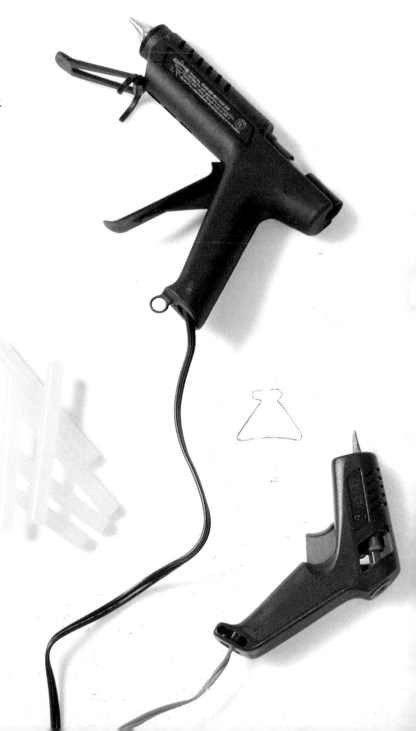

alternatives. There's no telling what could end up in your wreath: Christmas tree ornaments, garlic bulbs, apples, kids' toys, pomegranates…with a glue gun, anything's possible.

To use a glue gun, you simply plug it in, insert a glue stick, and wait a few minutes until the gun heats up enough to melt the glue. Then you aim the gun where you want the glue and pull the trigger. It's that simple. The only challenging part is avoiding the painful burns the hot glue can cause.

Glue guns come in two varieties (hot melt and low melt), and in two sizes (standard and mini). If you're new to wreath making and don't want to invest a lot of money, the mini glue gun will work just fine for about half to a quarter of the cost of the standard sizes. The benefits of the bigger glue guns include less time spent re-loading glue sticks and the availability of low-melt models whose glue melts at a temperature low enough to not cause severe burns. (The only negative to low melt glue guns is that they require special glue sticks that tend to be more expensive than regular glue sticks.)

GLUE GUN WORKING TIPS

◆ Spread out a protective layer of newspaper over your work area while your glue gun heats up. If your glue gun does not have a stand, find a glass plate or other non-flammable item to rest it on.

◆ Don't worry about the strands of dried glue that will appear as you work. Just gently pull them off when you've finished making the wreath.

◆ Play with angles and positions of your materials before you apply the first bit of glue.

◆ Hold larger items in place for at least a minute to ensure good bonding. Heavy items may need to be wired to the base first and then reinforced with hot glue.

◆ Keep a bowl of ice cubes near your working area to treat glue burns. If you're in a rush, tend to be on the clumsy side, or are working at an odd angle, you may want to wear a pair of thin garden gloves while you work.

◆ Unplug your glue gun whenever you leave its sight.

◆ If you have children in the house, be sure to store the glue gun in a safe place. You wouldn't want to find the cat's tail hot-glued to the tricycle or an antique vase to the refrigerator door.

FLORAL WIRE

Floral wire is one of those inexpensive, invaluable tools every crafter should have around the house. It's available in a variety of different thicknesses (referred to as gauge), in several different colors (brown, green, and silver), and is sold in pre-cut lengths and on spools. Thin and medium gauges of wire tend to be more flexible and thus easier to work with, although the thicker gauges can add some much-needed strength if you're trying to attach an unusually heavy item to a base. Always choose the color that will blend in best with the materials you're working with. Short lengths of floral wire are used to attach single items, such as bows, to wreath bases, whereas wire in spool-form is

used to attach small bouquets of dried or artificial flowers to single-wire wreath bases.

Why, you might ask, would you go to the trouble of cutting a length of wire, twisting it around the item, and then twisting it around the base (total elapsed time: 2½ minutes) if you could attach the same item in seconds with a dab of hot glue? Well, there are several good reasons. With some items you may wish to play with the precise angle and placement on the wreath, and with hot glue there's no time for playing. Other times, you may want to change a bow for a look more appropriate to the season, and if the bow is wired in place this is a very simple procedure: Just untwist the wires of the old bow and wire on the new bow. You may also choose wire as your attachment method when the item is something you cherish, such as a tree ornament that's been in the family for years—and you want to display it in a wreath but don't want it damaged from hot glue.

To wire a single item to a base, first cut a length of wire to approximately 12 inches (30 cm). Examine the item you want to attach to the base for an inconspicuous place to attach the wire. When you're wiring bows, for example, you can slip the wire through the center loop and no one will ever be the wiser.

If an inconspicuous place to attach the wire doesn't exist, you'll need to do some thinking about how you can disguise the wire once the item's on the wreath. With a teddy bear, for example, you can wire it around the neck and then cover the wire with a big bow. With other items, you may wish to disguise the wire by hot-gluing on small pieces of dried flowers or silk greenery.

Center the wire on the item and twist both ends of the wire together just under the item. Now choose the location on your base where you'd like the item to appear. Hold the item tightly against the base, and twist the wires together again until the tension is tight enough to hold the item in place. If you're not sure of the position, you can leave some slack in the wire while you play with angles. Reinforce heavy items with some hot glue and trim the wires with wire cutters when you've finished.

To attach natural materials such as herbs, flowers, and evergreens to a wire ring base, first cut the stems of the materials to a consistent length. Four-inch (10 cm) lengths work well with the standard 10- to 12-inch-

diameter (25 to 30 cm) wire ring bases; for smaller bases, trim the materials to 2½ or 3 inches (6 to 7 cm) in length; for larger bases, trim the materials to 5 or 6 inches (12 to 15 cm) in length. Arrange the materials into small bouquets of three to five stems per bouquet.

Position the first bouquet against the wire ring base and attach it by wrapping the spool wire around the stems of the materials and the base several times. Do not cut the spool wire. Position the next bouquet so its flowers or greenery overlap the wired stems of the previous bouquet and secure with several wraps of floral wire. Continue in this way until the entire base is covered. You can decide that your wreath is finished at this point or hot-glue single blooms onto the wired materials.

This method tends to create wreaths that are thinner and more delicate-looking than the traditional picked straw, but this is the ideal type of wreath to showcase the soft beauty of materials like pussy willow and German statice. If you decide you'd like a thicker wreath (or if you notice bare spots), you can hot-glue in additional stems of materials until you're satisfied with the fullness, taking care to position the stems at the same angle as the wired materials.

Floral wire can also be used to make small hanging hooks. To do this, make a half-inch (13 mm) wide loop in a piece of medium-gauge wire and twist several times. If you're working with a vine base, wire the ends of the loop to the vine and trim the wire. If you're working with a straw or foam base, trim both ends of the wire to half-inch lengths, then embed the ends into the back of the wreath and secure with hot glue.

FOAM & TUBES

If you find yourself feeling limited by the surface area of the standard wreath base, you can create three-dimensional effects in just about any shape with floral foam. Purchase the foam in large blocks in craft supply stores and then cut it down to size with a serrated knife. The foam will need to be big enough to accommodate the materials you plan to attach to it but not disproportionate to the size of the wreath base.

After you've cut down the foam, you will need to wire it to the base. Next, disguise the foam by

colors—if you were lucky. Today, you should skip the hardware store and shop for spray paint in a craft supply store. The color range in craft spray paints is magnificent—allowing you to match that pristine peach color on your sofa or the marvelous mauve wallpaper in your guest bedroom.

When it comes time to actually use the paint, keep in mind that more is not always better. If you're adding a blue tinge to a lotus pod, for example, add the color in single, light layers, allowing the paint to dry completely between layers. You'll probably find that the lotus pod, like most other natural materials, will look much better with some of its natural color showing through, instead of completely caked with blue. Also remember that it can be a lot of fun, not to mention create beautiful results, to work with several colors of spray paint. A branch of canella berries, for example, can be lightly misted with a layer of peach spray paint and then, after the

arranging moss over it and then securing the moss in place with floral pins. You can now insert long stems of dried materials through the moss and into the foam, or you can hot-glue materials directly to the moss.

For people who love to garden or who just love the look and smell of fresh flowers, floral tubes will seem like a marvel of crafting ingenuity. These plastic tubes resemble ordinary test tubes, except their lids have narrow slits in them for inserting flower stems and the base of the tubes have long narrow stems. The tubes' stems come to a sharp point, enabling you to insert them directly into a foam or straw base. Or, if you'd rather, you can simply hot-glue the tubes to the base, taking care to arrange other materials in the wreath to cover the plastic stems. Floral tubes aren't perfect: It's possible there may be some water leakage, so you should choose your display location with care.

PAINTS & POWDERS

If your design taste is somewhere in between the ardent naturalist and the synthetic superstar, these products will become your mainstay. Natural materials such as vines, seedpods, cones, seashells, and many other things can be jazzed up a bit in just minutes.

Spray paint is now an indispensable tool for many wreath makers. Not too many years ago, if you wanted some spray paint, you went down to your local hardware store and made your choice from eight or nine

paint has dried, misted again with gold spray paint. Larger items, such as pinecones, can be mentally divided into segments and then sprayed a different color in each segment, with the colors overlapping in some areas for a more natural look.

Another fun place to use spray paint is on vine wreath bases. Spray the paint onto the bare base in light layers, as you would with smaller items, and try to choose a color that will complement the colors in the wreath's materials or in the bow. If you have access to vine and feel up to the challenge of making your own vine bases, you may want to try your hand at the unusual base shown above. Spray paint five to seven vine lengths, each in a different color. Then, after you've woven them into a base, you have a rainbow effect that's completely custom-designed.

Gilding powder, as the name implies, is a metallic powder that can be used to add a gold glimmer to any number of objects. The powder is usually sold in small containers, and looks like the metallic eye make-up so popular in the '70s. Unlike spray paint, it's usually better to add gilding powder after your wreath is finished, to prevent it from rubbing off in all sorts of places where you do not want a tinge of gold. If, for instance, you rambunctiously hot-glued several rocks onto your wreath and now you're having second thoughts, the effect could easily be softened by just dabbing on a bit of gilding powder. This powder is also a great way to transform ordinary wreath materials into something special for the Christmas holidays or for formal occasions.

concern: Their wreaths were made for a bride to wear or to adorn a front door on a religious holiday. Today, several creative inventions from the floral industry—floral tubes and wet foam bases—make fresh flowers longer lasting and easier to work with. Floral tubes provide an unobtrusive water source for fresh flowers and can be re-filled as frequently as desired to keep the wreath looking nice. Page 24 provides more details on floral tubes and how to use them.

Wet foam bases are available in larger craft stores and through your florist. Usually a medium to dark green color, these bases are made from a soft, porous foam that easily absorbs water. Flowers will stay fresh-looking about the same length of time they would in a vase. To work with a wet foam base, simply soak it in water for a few minutes and then insert your flowers directly into the base. Stems should be cut at a sharp angle to make perforation easier and to encourage moisture absorption. If you have materials with weak stems, use a pencil tip to make small holes in the foam

MATERIALS

*W*REATH MATERIALS CAN BE AS traditional as evergreens or a novel as costume jewelry. Just keep an open mind and don't be afraid to try anything.

FRESH FLOWERS

Fresh flowers were chosen by the first wreath makers for their natural beauty, their fragrance, and their symbolic meanings. For these wreath makers, longevity was not a

before inserting the stems. Wet foam wreaths should be displayed on a table or other flat surface, with a protective layer of paper or plastic underneath to prevent water damage. Once the flowers wilt, simply remove the stems and re-use the base.

Several flowers dry so well that they can actually be hot-glued to a wreath base when they're fresh and then left to dry in place. You need to have some experience with flower drying before you try this, though, because not all flowers dry well, and some flowers shrink so much as they dry that they'll leave bare spots in the wreath. The following flowers make good choices for beginners because they're easy to dry and shrink very little: globe amaranth, strawflowers, and any kind of statice (annual, German, caspia, etc.).

One nice way to work is to hot-glue the above-mentioned flowers directly to a base and then use floral tubes to add exotic-looking flowers like proteas and iris. Wreaths can also be made from a mixture of fresh and dried materials. The only time you shouldn't mix and match is if you've dried some of your materials in silica gel, because the proximity to the moist, fresh flowers would probably make the silica-dried flowers re-absorb some of the fresh flowers' moisture and wilt.

Centuries ago, each flower and herb had a unique, symbolic meaning, and small gift bouquets were created as messages for loved ones (and ex loved ones!). Many of these flowers and herbs are still cultivated today, allowing wreath makers to create wreaths with symbolic meanings to celebrate special occasions. A birth wreath, for example, can be made from moss (maternal love), honeysuckle (sweetness of disposition), pussy willow (unrealized promise), and bachelor's buttons (single blessedness). A wedding wreath can be made from roses (love), rosemary (remembrance and fidelity), sage (wisdom), chamomile (energy in adversity), and globe amaranth (unfading affection).

DRIED FLOWERS

Dried flowers and herbs are a mainstay in traditional wreaths. They're almost as beautiful as fresh-cut blooms, but they last for years. You can purchase small bouquets of dried flowers in most craft supply stores,

and often in a wider range of color choices than Mother Nature offers because the dried flowers have been soaked in dye baths. If you tend to have trouble with allergies, though, you'll need to sniff before you purchase, since many commercially marketed dried flowers are imported and have been treated with insect repellent. (No sense making a gorgeous wreath only to find out it makes you sneeze!) Also, never display a dried flower wreath on a wall that receives lots of sunlight or the beautiful colors will fade.

A simple, inexpensive alternative to purchasing your dried flowers and herbs is to dry them from your garden. There's nothing mysterious about the process: All flowers and herbs will dry after they've been picked. The problem is, not all of them will look attractive enough to use in a wreath. Many turn brown. Others retain their color yet shrivel up into an unattractive mass. Some keep their shape perfectly but shrink so much during the drying process that you have to dry a lot of extra materials. The paragraphs that follow explain the basic techniques for harvesting and drying flowers and herbs from your own garden, as well as descriptions of flowers and herbs that almost always dry well. The drying process is complete when the flower or herb feels like a flake of breakfast cereal.

To dry your own flowers, you'll first have to harvest them. Choose a sunny day, after the morning dew has dried and well after a rain shower. Avoid picking materials with damage from insects, and pick a lot more than you anticipate needing to accommodate the natural reduction in size due to shrink-age. Pick flowers in several stages of bloom—from bud form to fully opened—so you can discover which stage holds its color, shape, and size the best.

Most materials can be dried with one of several air-drying techniques. Hanging, the oldest of these techniques, involves grouping several stems of the same flower or herb together, securing their stems together with string or a rubber band, and then hanging them upside down in a dark, dry location. The flowers are hung upside down so the blooms will dry in a more natural position. Another air-drying method, known as screen or rack drying, involves spreading single blooms

or leaves on a wire screen that has been arranged so there's ventilation on all sides. Drying times tend to vary, depending on the type of plant and how moist it was when it was harvested. Five to 15 days is an average range.

Flowers can also be dried with desiccants by layering blooms in one of several moisture-absorbing substances, such as borax, kitty litter, sand, or silica gel. Silica gel is the most expensive of these desiccants, but its granules are lighter in weight than the other desiccants and tend not to crush delicate blooms. Check the progress of your blooms every few days to prevent overdrying, and avoid leaving already-dry blooms in a moist area such as the bathroom to prevent them from reabsorbing moisture.

With a new drying method known as microwave drying, the moisture in some varieties of flowers can be removed in just minutes by cooking them with silica gel. Because the moisture in flowers can vary so much from variety to variety and even from day to day, and because the wattages in microwaves vary so much, you will need to allow extra flowers and time for experimenting, but once you perfect the times (and make note of them!) you can dry flowers in minutes for the rest of the summer.

To dry flowers in the microwave, first layer the bottom of a microwave-safe container with a thin layer of silica gel. Arrange the flowers in a single layer so that their sides do not touch and cover them with another thin layer of silica gel. Cook on a medium setting for 2½ minutes and allow a standing time of ten minutes. If your flowers are overdried, start again with fresh materials and reduce the time in 30-second intervals. If the flowers are still not dry, add time in 15-second intervals.

Following is a brief list of some of the most popular flowers and herbs used in wreath making.

Bee Balm should be harvested early in the blooming cycle and can be air-dried on a screen.

Blue Salvia (also known as Indigo Spires) can be air-dried by hanging upside down in small bundles. The delicate blooms should be handled gently to prevent breakage.

Celosia, both the plumed and crested varieties, holds its color and shape well, and can be air-dried by hanging upside down after the foliage has been

removed. Celosia should always be harvested early in the morning to prevent matting.

Dusty Miller is popular for its silvery foliage, which maintains its shape perfectly. The leaves should be spread out on a screen rack to dry and turned frequently.

Roses can be air-dried by hanging stems of just-opened blooms upside down in small bundles. Roses in any stage of bloom can also be dried in a desiccant.

'Silver King' and *'Silver Queen'* *Artemisias* are dried for their silvery foliage, which makes a nice background material in wreaths. Hang the stems upside down if straight lines are desired, or stand them upright in a bottle if curved lines are desired.

Baby's Breath dries quickly by hanging upside down in small, loose bunches.

Globe Amaranth's colorful blooms make wonderful wreath accents, and they air-dry in just a few days on a drying rack.

Larkspur should be harvested for drying when the majority of the flowers on the stalk have opened, and then hung upside down in small bundles to dry. Dried larkspur ranges in color from pale pink, lavender, and cream to deep purple.

Statices are very popular in wreaths because they are so easy to grow and dry. Just hang them upside down for a few days and they're ready to use.

Strawflowers can be dried by spreading the blooms on a rack or hanging the stems upside down in small bundles. They hold their colors wonderfully, and come in all sorts of brilliant shades from purple and red to bright orange and yellow.

EVERGREENS & GREENERY

Humans have always been fascinated with evergreens and greenery, perhaps because we see them as nature's promise—present even in the coldest of winters—that life will continue. Early civilizations revered

evergreens and greenery so much that they made garlands from laurel and olive greenery to celebrate the victories of the first Olympians.

Wreaths made completely from evergreens or greenery form a versatile backdrop for adding seasonal accents. In the spring and summer, tuck water tubes filled with fresh flowers into the foliage and add a festive floral bow. As fall approaches, change the bow, remove the flowers, and wire in some decorative squash. In the winter, replace the bow with a bright red one, replace the squash with some tree ornaments, and tuck in a few sprigs of berries.

Evergreens and greenery also work surprisingly well as filler in wreaths made from knick-knacks, flowers, herbs, and unusual props.

Wreaths made from evergreens and greenery can be assembled in several ways. With strong-stemmed evergreens such as firs, you can simply cut the stems at an angle and insert them directly into a foam or straw base. Materials with more delicate stems can be wired to a wire ring base or attached in small groups to floral picks. Individual leaves can also be arranged around a wreath and hot-glued in place.

Many varieties of evergreens and greenery can be purchased in craft stores and discount marts. These materials have usually been preserved with glycerin, which means they will retain much of their natural color and shape. Materials can be glycerin-preserved at home by filling a small container with three parts water and one part glycerin. Then make several angular cuts in the evergreens' stems and stand them upright in the liquid. As time passes, the evergreens will absorb the glycerin mixture through their stems. The process usually takes about two weeks. Several varieties of leaves also do well with glycerin-preserving, although their fleshier stems may require a higher ratio of glycerin to water. Other materials, such as boxwood, ivy, bay, and mint, can be used fresh in a wreath and then left on the wreath to dry in place.

BERRIES

Berries have been the unfortunate victims of several negative stereotypes among wreath makers. First, it's long been assumed that berries are only for holiday wreaths. Second, crafters often assume that all berries are red. But as the wreaths in this book demonstrate so beautifully, berries make a wonderful wreath material any time of the year, echoing the round wreath shape with their small circle clusters and providing a bit of colorful pizazz.

You'll find berries in almost as many colors as flowers. Pepperberries are a common choice because they're often available in larger craft stores and from florists, and because they come in pink and red varieties. Berries can also be found in foliage, such as

Silver Dollar' eucalyptus, whose berries are a light green.

Other popular craft berries, such as the canella berry, come in almost every color in the rainbow, thanks to the magic of commercial dyes.

Silk and plastic berries are also good choices, especially if you have young children in the house. Even the most ardent naturalist will be amazed at how natural these commercial inventions appear, and their fantastic color range is often difficult to resist.

The easiest way to attach berries to a wreath is to hot-glue or floral pin them in small bunches. Unless you have a penchant for detail, it's best to save the individual berries for potpourri. (If you insist on adding individual berries to a wreath, however, don't invite burns by using a hot glue gun.)

CONES, NUTS, & SEEDPODS

Renowned for their appearances over the years in holiday wreaths, pinecones, nuts, and seedpods are now used in wreaths for all seasons. Many craft stores offer some very unique selections, although an attentive stroll through almost any wooded area is likely to yield an equally interesting variety. Large flowering trees, such as the magnolia, are also a good source for interesting seed heads and should be checked in the fall. If you choose to collect your own materials, it's probably a good idea to bake them in a 200° F (93° C) oven for 30 minutes to kill any insects.

These natural materials can be used without altering their natural colors or they can be sprayed with your favorite craft paint. Metallics seem to work especially well on these rustic materials, perhaps because of the contrast. For just a touch of jazz, consider dabbing on a little bit of gilding powder to the petals of cones or the edges of nuts and seedpods. Pinecone flowers can be made by placing large cones on their sides and

slicing them in inch-wide (2½ cm) slices. Public perception is often that pinecones, nuts, and seedpods are rough and rustic in nature. Many of them, though, such as miniature hemlock cones and love-in-a-mist, are very small and delicate.

Cones, seedpods, and nuts can be attached to wreath bases in several ways. To wire a cone to a base, slip a length of medium-gauge floral wire through the bottom petals of the cone and twist the wires together until tightened. Then wrap the wires around the base and twist again. Extremely heavy cones may need to be reinforced with several dabs of hot glue. Smaller seedpods and heads can be attached to bases with craft picks. Just hot-glue the flat end of the pick to the item and then insert the tapered end into the base. Smaller materials can be simply hot-glued directly to the base.

MOSSES

As a decorative material, moss is often the small touch that ties an entire wreath together. Moss is still one of the last strongholds of nature—it can't be molded from plastic, paper, or silk, as flowers often are. It adds a nice sense of texture to the wreath as well as making the finished wreath look more natural.

Moss also makes wonderful filler material, especially with larger wreaths, when finding enough materials to cover the whole base can be challenging and expensive. Other times, a wreath is made from materials so large that the gaps, however inevitable, are disruptive to the beauty of the finished wreath if left unattended. If the gaps are small, you can usually just tuck small clumps of moss into the spaces without using a glue gun. If the gaps are large, however, you'll probably need to use a glue gun. Be sure to use a pencil or other object to press the moss into the glue to prevent burns.

Several varieties of mosses are sold in small packages in craft stores. Remember, if you opt to pick

your own moss, you should find out which varieties, if any, are endangered in your area.

RIBBONS & BOWS

The right bow has the power to transform an average-looking wreath into an extraordinary one, so it makes sense to learn as much as you can about them. The wide range of patterns, colors, and textures available—from polka dots to paisleys, from pastels to

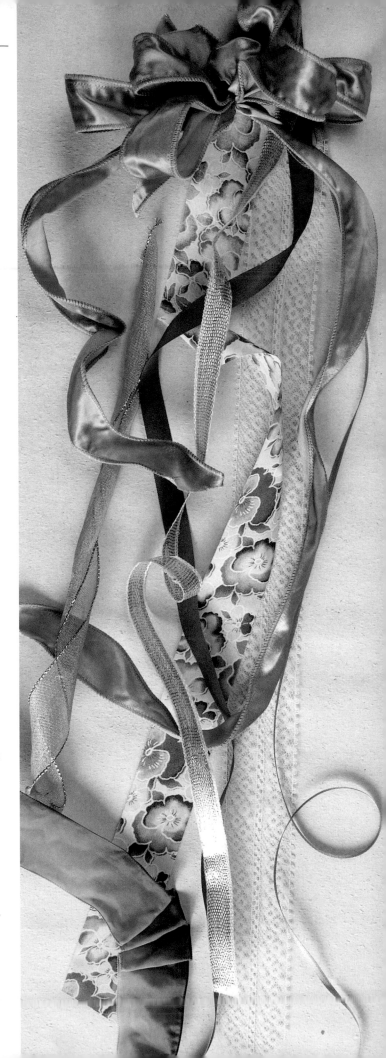

brights, from velvet to raffia—lets you control the style of your wreath by your choice of ribbon. A large bow may be the wreath's focal point, while a smaller bow often looks like just another material in the wreath. Once they've been attached to the base, bows can be decorated with dried flowers and other materials, or left as is.

Following are brief descriptions of some of the more popular bow materials.

- ◆ *Satin ribbon's* main strength is that it's sold in so many widths that it's easy to make the perfect size bow for your wreath, no matter how big or small it is. Satin ribbon also makes an attractive material to cover foam and straw bases. The ribbon can be too slippery for crafters just learning to tie bows.
- ◆ *Cotton ribbon* makes a good ribbon for beginners because crease marks can be ironed out with a hot iron so the ribbon can be used again. For admirers of the country look, the lively prints make cotton ribbon a good choice.
- ◆ *Paper ribbon* is sold in long spools and then unrolled before using. It ties easily into simple bows and can be re-shaped if the bow is crushed. Paper ribbon can be reused, so it's a good material for beginners.
- ◆ *Velvet ribbon* adds a very formal and traditional look to a wreath, but it's easily crushed and not re-usable if you make a mistake.
- ◆ *Wired ribbon* (also known as French ribbon) is lined with rows of thin-gauge wire on its wrong side so it can be shaped and re-shaped as often as you like.
- ◆ *Cellophane ribbon* adds a hint of holiday glitz to a wreath, and it's an easy material for beginners to work with. The metallic colors may be too bright for some people.
- ◆ *Raffia strands* adds a natural flair to any wreath. It's easy to work with and accepts dye well.
- ◆ *Lace ribbon* is the ideal choice for wedding and anniversary wreaths. If it's not stiff enough for the loops to hold their shape, dip it in liquid fabric stiffener before you tie the bow.

If you're working with very contemporary or free-flowing natural materials—such as mushrooms, cooking

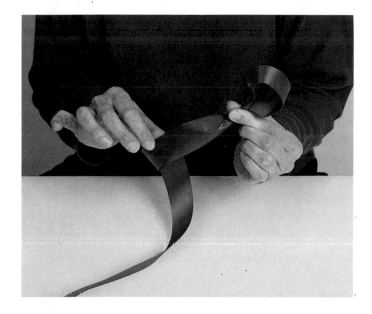

utensils, etc—a large bow may look out of place. Wired ribbon (also known as French ribbon) can be looped, twisted, and curled around a base to create a free-flowing look. The ribbon's wire enables it to hold these whimsical shapes for a look that's completely natural. Ribbon loops and streamers can be the first or last material secured to the base. If the wreath is for the holidays, you can secure the ribbon to the base every few inches (7 to 10 cm) with a long sewing pin; if the ribbon is to become a permanent part of the wreath, it can be secured with small amounts of hot glue. Paper, cellophane, satin, and cotton ribbons can also be worked around a wreath this way, but the loops and twists will need to be more condensed, and you'll need to secure them to their bases in closer intervals.

If you plan to create an arrangement on one side of the wreath and leave the remaining surface areas undecorated, you can cover a base (usually foam or straw) with ribbon. Start by securing one end of the ribbon to the base with a floral or long sewing pin. Then begin wrapping the ribbon around the base at a slight angle with just enough overlap to prevent the base from showing. Secure the ribbon to the base every few inches (7 to 10 cm) with another pin. It's also a good idea to cover a foam or straw base with ribbon if your materials are so large that there will be large space gaps between them. Narrow strips of fabric can be substituted for the ribbon if desired.

A bow is simply a symmetrical arrangement of ribbon loops that's embellished with streamers. The number and size of the loops and the width of the ribbon determines the look of the finished bow. Learning to tie a bow is a simple process, but you'll need to practice quite a bit before your bows resemble a professional's. The directions that follow explain how to make a bow by first creating a streamer, then constructing two medium-size loops, then two long loops, then two short loops, and finally two more medium-size loops.

First, cut an 8-inch (20 cm) length of ribbon at an angle to form the first two streamers. Crimp the middle of the streamer and hold it tightly between your thumb and index finger. Then make the third streamer by crimping an un-cut length of ribbon about 4 inches (10 cm) in from one end.

Keeping the streamers held tightly, form a medium-size loop (about 3 to 4 inches, 7.5 to 10 cm), making sure the right side of the ribbon is facing outward. (Note: A loop consists of two parts, a top loop and a bottom loop.) Now make another medium-size loop, positioning it so it's next to the previous loop and not on top of it. Be careful to keep the center tightly crimped.

Form two larger loops about an inch (2.5 cm) longer than the medium-size loops. Now create two smaller loops about an inch smaller than the medium-size loops and position them on top of the large loops. Add two more medium-size loops adjacent to the large loops.

Switch the bow to your other hand, holding tightly to prevent your work from unraveling. Twist a length of thin-gauge floral wire around the streamers and the loops. Trim the un-cut length of ribbon to match the length and angle of the other streamers.

Cover the wire with a short length of ribbon looped around the center and hot-glued in place on the back side of the bow. Fluff and shape the bow by pulling the streamers and rolling your finger around the inside of the loops in the order in which they were added.

SILK, PAPER, & PLASTIC

In wreath making, natural isn't always better. Sometimes silk, paper, and plastic materials just make more sense. If you plan to display your wreath outdoors, silks and plastics won't be damaged by the elements. If you plan to hang your wreath on an indoor wall that receives direct sunlight, the colors in silk and paper flowers will not fade like those in dried flowers. And, speaking of color, these materials are always available in popular design colors such as mauve, peach, and country blue. When you shop for silks, papers, and plastics, make your choices carefully: Look for blooms that can arranged in more natural-looking shapes and for stems lined with thin-gauge wire so they can be curved to suit your wreath base.

Flowers are the most common of these materials, but berries and greenery are quickly gaining in popularity. You may remember plastic leaves as being thick, glossy, and utterly tacky, but manufacturers have responded to the preferences of crafters and improved their products considerably. If you're forced to use plastic berries because of young children in

the house, look for the new varieties that have multiple shades of coloring for a more natural appeal, instead of the glossy, prefabricated look of the past.

Attaching these materials to a base is fast and simple. Long stems of materials like ivy or other greenery can be wrapped around the base and secured in intervals with floral pins or hot glue. Blooms with a strong stem can be inserted directly into a foam or straw base, or dabbed at their ends with hot glue and inserted into a vine base. Wire cutters can be used to clip single blooms and smaller stems of foliage from their main stems, and the blooms can then be arranged around the wreath and hot-glued in place.

KITCHEN GOODIES

While they may look quite ordinary on the grocery market shelves and in your fruit dish at home, fruits and vegetables add an unexplainable burst of excitement to wreaths. Their natural colors, textures, and shapes blend in perfectly with flowers and other natural materials, and you can also make wreaths exclusively from these materials. Fruits and vegetables also make spectacular table wreaths for centerpieces, and the materials allow for all kinds of design flexibility. Instead of covering a foam base with ribbon, for instance, you can cover it with bright purple radicchio leaves, securing them in place as needed with floral pins.

The only real trick to working successfully with fruits and vegetables is to keep scale in the forefront of your mind as you assemble the wreath. If you're working with a 10-inch (25 cm) base, for example, chances are that an artichoke would look out of place because it is proportionately too big. Likewise, single grapes would get lost on a 30-inch (75 cm) wreath base, but larger clusters would not.

Two considerations should be taken into account before you decide which method to use to attach your materials. The first consideration is the weight and size of the item. Small, light items such as mushrooms or radishes can be hot-glued in place; medium-weight items such as potatoes and apples can be attached with craft picks; large, lightweight materials such as grape clusters and lettuce leaves can be attached with floral pins; and heavier items such as broccoli and squashes may need a combination of wiring and hot glue to stay in place. The second consideration is whether you want the materials in your finished wreath to be edible, in which case you obviously want to avoid using hot glue.

Keep in mind that the weight of all these fruits and vegetables can add up, making your wreath too heavy to hang unless you've used a wire-reinforced base.

Also, remember that you don't have to fill every square inch with fruits and vegetables—just tuck in sprigs of Spanish moss for a totally natural look.

Raiding the kitchen cupboards is a sure way to produce innovative wreaths. Cinnamon sticks, star anise, garlic bulbs, chili peppers, bay leaves, nutmeg, allspice berries, cloves, and even small pieces of candy all look nice in wreaths. Arrange a bag of assorted whole nuts around a foam wreath base, hot-glue them in place, dab on a little gilding powder, and you've got a terrific wreath. Dried beans are another versatile wreath material—you'll need a lot of patience and a steady hand to avoid hot-glue burns, but the terrific designs are more than worth the effort. Bows made from raffia seem to look especially nice on wreaths made from kitchen materials.

connoisseur, for example, would love a wreath made from wine corks. (Don't worry—many craft stores sell wine corks by the bag, so you won't end up with shelves of un-corked wine.) A chef would enjoy a wreath made from cooking utensils. (Again, you won't have to spend a lot—just shop garage sales or dime stores for bargains.) The same type of wreath could be made for a gardener, with digging tools, old gloves, and some miniature clay pots.

At Christmas time, a trip to the local discount mart for a box of ornaments and sundry tree trimmings will provide more than enough materials to make lots of wreaths. Or, if you've spent years collecting ornaments for a perfectly coordinated tree, you can just borrow a few ornaments and find some matching ribbon so the tree will match the wreath. Even heirloom ornaments can be showcased in a wreath; wire them gently in place or tuck them into the greenery so they won't be damaged. Tinsel, garlands, and beads can also be looped around a wreath base with stunning results.

Don't be afraid of using larger items in a wreath. Hats, shoes, sunglasses, car parts, old music instruments, sheet music, bells, figurines, children's toys, dolls, and stuffed animals all have potential as wreath materials. These larger items, often referred to as

NATURAL ACCENTS

If you have an open mind, Mother Nature offers a wonderful assortment of wreath materials. Fungi, lichens, sea shells, feathers, and bee and wasp nests are just a few of the possibilities. Offer a neighborhood child a dollar for a bag of such goodies, and you'll be amazed at the results. These items work equally well as background materials or as accents, so quantity isn't really important. Small, lightweight materials can be hot-glued in place. Feathers can be inserted by their stems directly into a foam base.

INSPIRATIONS

When looking for innovative wreath materials, it often helps to search the room where you plan to hang the wreath. If you're making a wreath for your sewing room, for instance, thread spools, fabric scraps, embroidery floss, thimbles, and bobbins are all fair game. For a wreath you plan to hang over your dressing table, old jewelry and handkerchiefs can be borrowed. And for the bathroom, consider making a wreath from fragrant bath soaps in assorted shapes and colors, accented with a bow tied from a decorative hand towel.

The next time a birthday rolls around for someone who has virtually everything, consider making a custom wreath with materials from their favorite hobby. A wine

props, can easily establish a theme for a wreath. Because of their size, they are usually attached to the wreath's base with a combination of wire and hot glue. Junk drawers, closets, and garage sales are good sources for these materials.

After you've chosen a prop and found a base large enough to accommodate it, it makes sense to attach it to the base before you begin adding other materials for several reasons. First, this order enables you to arrange other materials around the prop so that it looks like a natural, integral part of the wreath, instead of like some dumb thing someone stuck on top at the last minute. Second, if you wait until last to add the prop, its size and weight will probably damage the smaller, more delicate materials in the wreath.

DESIGN

ESIGN IS ONE OF THOSE TERRIBLE WORDS that can strike fear in a crafter's heart. A wreath that is well designed, though, is just pleasing to the eye. That's all there is to it. A well-designed wreath can be excruciatingly simple or very complex; the materials can be very expensive or freebies from Mother Nature. As long as you work with attractive materials, the circle shape of the wreath base will help ensure a beautiful finished wreath. The ideas that follow should give you several approaches if you're still nervous, although you may find that many of your choices will be dictated by the types and quantities of materials you have available.

TIPS OF THE TRADE

◆ If you're attaching materials to a straw, foam, or moss base with picks or floral pins, be sure to position the materials at an angle, and continue positioning the materials at this same angle all the way around the wreath, rotating the wreath as you work.

◆ When you're hot-gluing accent materials to a wreath, arrange them at different depths and angles in the background material.

◆ Don't be concerned about making the wreath completely symmetrical and perfectly balanced. Some

materials, such as fresh flowers, vegetables, and ribbons look better spilling over the confines of the base.

◆ When using large props or other objects, remember that the visual "weight" of the object may make the wreath look unbalanced. Offset the prop by arranging several smaller materials on the opposite side of the wreath.

METHODS

Many wreath designers use a solid background material with occasional accents as a design template. The background material can be a single item, such as a background of Fraser fir for a holiday wreath, or it can be made from several different materials that are the same color. The type of background material you choose will determine the feel of the wreath. A background of the statice known as caspia, for example, will create a delicate, whimsical-looking wreath, whereas a background of something more sturdy, such as pinecones or evergreens, will have a more rustic look.

The best wreath designers choose their accent materials with care. Ideally, these materials should be in a color that contrasts or complements the background color, and since you'll need so few of them, it's worth the trouble to search out something really special. Look for items with intricate detail or special meaning. Accent materials are usually added last to prevent their being damaged by heavier background materials. They are usually attached with hot glue, although floral pins or wire are also options if you're not in a rush. For best effect, be sure to position the materials at different depths and angles.

The multiple surface areas of a wreath base can be outlined in different materials for stunning effects. The inner and outer edges of the base can be picked with a simple material such as German statice, leaving the top surface area to be covered with colorful, contrasting materials. The inner and outer edges can also be covered with different colors and varieties of materials, and the top surface area can be subdivided into two or three areas and outlined as well. There are no rules: look closely at your materials and let them dictate your choices.

Another style of wreath making is the hodgepodge design. Successful hodgepodge wreaths appear to have lots of materials attached in random order. Actually, though, the order probably wasn't random at all. To make a hodgepodge design, first sort your materials by size, weight, and delicacy. Arrange the largest and heaviest materials around the base first and secure them in place with wire and/or hot glue. Next, fill in gaps with other materials, taking care to space out different colors and shapes more or less equally around the base. Add the smallest, most delicate materials last, positioning them to showcase their beauty and also to fill in any bare spots. Since there is no single focal point to this type of wreath, you can place the bow anywhere you like.

Cones & Pods

OFFERING A MYRIAD OF beautiful shapes and textures, cones and seed pods are nature's gift to wreath crafters. Work them in to silk, dried flower, or evergreen wreaths, or use them in combination with asymmetrical twigs and branches. The more sizes and varieties, the better. Cones and seed pods can be enhanced with color— just give them a light spray of gold or copper paint and use them in your favorite celebration wreath. An interesting variety of cones and pods can be purchased in craft stores. If you chose to collect your own, be sure to ward off pests by baking your collection in a 200° F (93° C) oven for about 30 minutes, turning halfway through.

Forest Harvest

RENOWNED FOR THEIR APPEARANCES over the years in holiday wreaths, pinecones, nuts, and seedpods are now used in wreaths for all seasons. Many craft stores offer some very unique selections, although an attentive stroll through almost any wooded area is likely to yield an equally interesting variety.

To make this wreath, wire your favorite cones and pods to a wire ring base. Fill in gaps by tucking in small sprigs of moss.

Designer: **Cynthia Gillooly**

Rustic

NATURAL TWIGS AND BRANCHES create an airy, whimsical quality for this wall display. To make the wreath, hot-glue stems of twigs and branches into a twig base until you've created the desired fullness. Spray small pinecones and silk ivy with gold paint, then spray large silk leaves with splatters of gold paint. Hot-glue the gold cones and foliage into the wreath at attractive intervals.

Designer: **Anthea Masters**

Keepsake Wreath

*T*HERE'S NO RULE THAT REQUIRES YOU TO leave an empty space in the middle of a wreath. Why not use it as an opportunity to frame a treasured keepsake like this ceramic Father Christmas, which lends old-world charm to this lovely Yuletide creation.

To make the wreath, wire old St. Nick into a purchased vinyl blue spruce wreath and hot glue in some cones, dried pomegranates, pepperberries, silk flowers, iridescent clear glass balls, and tiny homemade Christmas packages. Add a large bow with hot glue and loop excess ribbon loosely through the greenery.

Designer: **Janet Frye**

Bountiful Bouquet

*A*FEELING OF WILD NATURAL GROWTH, OF seed pods ready to drop, of berries to be gathered for the coming winter all combine in this striking autumn creation.

To make the wreath, weave stems of fresh-cut bittersweet into a vine wreath base. Next, hot-glue groupings of preserved oak leaves, dried mushrooms, lamb's wool, okra, mahogany pods, plastic berries, globe amaranth, straw flowers, and protea. To finish, wire the bow to the top of the wreath and weave the ribbon streamers down and around the sides of the wreath.

Designer: **Diane Weaver**

Touch-Tempting Teasel

𝓘N CERTAIN LIGHTS, THIS HANDSOME TEASEL wreath looks like it's made of feathers, which is ironic because one touch tells you it's prickly, not downy. (The other magic thing about this wreath is what happens when you add a red or green bow.) Be very careful working with teasel. You may want to use sandpaper to remove the briars on the stems.

To make the wreath, start with a straw base wrapped in green plastic. Brush the teasel heads lightly if small particles are caught in the texture. Spray each head with silver paint, then hold the teasel upright and spray again to cover the little indentations. Pick the teasel heads. Working from the top of the wreath, insert the teasel into the base. (Long-nose pliers work great for grasping the pick and stem and helping to push the teasel into the base.) Position the teasel heads so they point down each side of wreath. Allow a space at the top for a bow. Make a full bow and wire it on. Finally, spray the Queen Anne's lace and glue it into place.

Designer:
KIT MEEKLEY

Special Occasion Wreath

*F*LOWERS, CONES, AND RIBBON IN GOLD AND ivory colors create a wreath that's ideal for wedding, anniversary, and winter holiday celebrations.

To make the wreath, begin by spraying a grapevine wreath base, half a dozen pine cones, and several stems of silk ivy with gold paint. After the paint has dried, hot-glue silk cabbage roses and silk hydrangeas to the base. Next, arrange a length of wired ribbon loosely around the base. Hot-glue the cones and ivy to the base. Fill in any gaps with small sprigs of hydrangea.

Designer: **Anthea Masters**

Earth Tones

A STUDY IN BROWN, THIS CONE-AND-NUT wreath displays the intricate patterns supplied by nature, that master designer.

Gather cones soon after they fall from the tree or simply pluck them off. Test by squeezing: If the cone doesn't crumble, it's usable. Nuts are equally variable: buckeyes, acorns, hazelnuts, even peach pits.

Bake all nuts for 25 minutes at 200° F (79 C°), and clip any stems from cones. For variety in color, cones can be soaked in a strong bleach solution and allowed to dry. To make the flowers, cut cones carefully crosswise and remove any seeds that spoil the shape.

To make the wreath, cut a piece of pegboard into a wreath shape, then just wire the cones and attach them to the base. Hot-glue nuts around the wreath at attractive intervals. Clip the long wires on the back and attach a wire hanger. To prevent the back wires from scratching surfaces, cover it with felt.

For the Birds

T HIS ARTIFICIAL HOLIDAY wreath in traditional red and green is given a nontraditional place of honor on a feathered friend's front door. Start with an artificial evergreen wreath. Wire the pinecones together in clusters of three and then wire the groupings evenly spaced to the wreath base. Wire on grape clusters between the pinecone clusters. Make five red raffia bows and wire them to the base near the grapes. Attach Virginia creeper to floral picks and wire them to the base. For that wintery look, glue on frosted branches.

Designer: **Julianne Bronder**

Designer:
Wana Henry

Fruit-n-Flowers

A MEDLEY OF COLORFUL DRIED fruits, flowers, and seed pods creates a wreath with great depth and appeal.

To make the wreath, attach pomegranates, dried mushrooms, dried okra, love-in-a-mist pods, blue salvia, and globe amaranth to floral picks. Insert the heavier items into a natural vine or twig wreath base, then begin adding the lighter items. Hot-glue dried orange slices at varying depths and angles, then fill in any gaps with small sections of hydrangea blooms.

Designer: **Diane Weaver**

My Favorite Things

*S*ERENDIPIDY CAN BE A WREATH DESIGNERS best friend. Just place an interesting assortment of your favorite wreath materials on a table in front of you and explore the possibilities.

To make this wreath, hot-glue short stems of fresh cedar around the outside edge of a small vine base. Next, cut small cones in half to create cone flowers and hot-glue them around the center-top surface of the wreath. Fill in the gaps with rose buds, moss, and bay leaves, then hot-glue a spicy clove onto each bay leaf.

To store the wreath from year to year, place it in a box slightly larger than the wreath and gently cover it on all sides with tissue paper. Continue packing paper around the wreath until you do not hear any movement when you shake the box.

Designer. **Corinne Erb**

The Bird's Nest

*R*ICH AUTUMN COLORS AND WHIMSICAL swirls of raffia create this naturally beautiful door display.

To make the wreath, wire a purchased or found bird's nest to the bottom left side of a grapevine base and hot-glue a feather under it. Next, hot-glue large silk blooms around the wreath, then add stems of silk berries, natural vines, and seed pods around the wreath. Finish by hot-gluing small sprigs of hydrangea to fill in any gaps and weaving lengths of raffia around the wreath.

Designer: **Anthea Masters**

Ribbon-Wrapped Wreath

WRAPPING A PLAIN STRAW BASE IN TWO colors of ribbon makes a subtle backdrop for a dramatic bouquet of fresh hemlock and pine cones.

To make the wreath, wrap a straw base with red velvet and green satin ribbons, securing occasionally with floral pins or hot glue. Make bouquets of hemlock stems and attach them to floral picks. Insert the picks into the straw base, then attach the cones with wire and picks. Finish with a dramatic bow.

Designer: **Fred Gaylor**

To Dye For

*O*F YOU LIKE YOUR NATURAL WREATHS WITH a little more color, consider dying some of your natural materials. To begin, wire pinecones all the way around the outer edge of a wire base. Next, fill in the inner edge of the wreath with wired pods and more cones, then spray the entire wreath with a coat of polyurethane finish. After the finish has dried, hot-glue an assortment of dyed flowers, wheat, and wood shavings in the gaps, then add a bow as a final touch.

Designer: **Kit Meckley**

Precious Pinecone Wreath

*P*INECONES—ONE OF NATURE'S MOST beautiful throwaways—make wonderful wreaths. Because of the relatively large size of cones, these wreaths go together quickly, giving you extra time to experiment with ribbons, flowers, nuts, and other decorative acumen. (They make an ideal project for restless children.) And, if you become bored with the simple shapes of the cones, try cutting cones horizontally to make pinecone flowers.

To make this wreath, hot-glue a variety of cones, nuts, and seed pods to a heart-shaped wire ring base. Tuck small pieces of moss in the gaps to prevent the base from showing and to round out the shape. Finish with a small bird's nest instead of the traditional bow.

Designer: **Chris Rankin**

Just Add Veggies

*C*OLORFUL SILK VEGETABLES in a variety of colors and sizes look great when paired with natural seed pods. To make the wreath, wire the vegetables in place from their back sides at interesting angles around a grapevine base. Finish by hot-gluing clusters of seed pods (mimosa tree pods were used in this wreath), silk berries, and silk foliage around the vegetables.

Designer: **Anthea Masters**

Winter Solstice

*N*ATURAL COLORS AND FRAGRANCES combine in this lush winter wreath. To make the wreath, create small bouquets of dried canella berries, German statice, gypsophilia, dyed yarrow, dusty miller, pearly everlasting, glycerin-preserved fraser fir, and pine cones. Attach the bouquets to floral picks, then insert the picks into the base, beginning with the sturdier materials (such as the fraser fir) and finishing with the most delicate ones. Finish with a bow or holiday ornaments.

Designer: **Nancy McCauley**

Raise the Red Lanterns

*C*HINESE-LANTERNS (PHYSALIS), ALSO CALLED ground-cherries, make interesting additions to wreaths. Members of the nightshade family, this group of plants also includes tomatoes, peppers, and petunias. The genus name means bladder, a fitting reference to the papery pods that contain the plant's seeds.

To make the wreath, first wire a length of ribbon to the upper left portion of a grapevine wreath base. Glue the ends of the ribbon to the edges of the wreath. Next, make small bouquets, each of sweet Annie, santolina blooms, Chinese-lanterns, and baby's breath. Add a birch branch to each bouquet and secure each bouquet with several wraps of floral tape. Place the bouquets on top of the ribbon, facing the ends outward. Wire the bouquets in place and cover the stems with a bow.

Designer: **Alyce Nadeau**

Dried Flowers & Herbs

RIED FLOWERS AND herbs are easy to find in most craft stores, but they're also easy to prepare yourself with fresh cuttings from the garden. Many flowers and herbs—including German statice, caspia, baby's breath, strawflowers, and bay, just to name a few—can be placed in a wreath when fresh cut and will dry in place with little or no change in appearance. Some dried flowers and herbs, such as roses and mint, will even retain some of their wonderful fragrances after they've been dried. To extend the lifespan of dried flower and herb leaves, be sure to display them away from direct sunlight, which can cause them to fade and crumble.

Forever Springtime

*P*EACH AND WHITE ANNUAL STATICE MAKE a delightful springtime combination. To make the wreath, start with a base made of dried German statice. Hot-glue clusters of native blooms in random locations all around the base, leaving spaces between the clusters to fill with peach strawflowers and pink globe amaranths. Add accents of blackberry seed pods and marjoram. For a greater sense of depth and color contrast, insert bay leaves intermittently around the outer and inner rings of the wreath, adding just a few in the center as well.

Designer: **Jane Dicus**

Tapestry Wreath

A TAPESTRY-PRINT BOW BLENDS SHADES of grey, ivory, and pink blooms into a truly enchanting wreath. To make the wreath, wire small bouquets of silver-king artemisia to a wire base, then hot-glue individual blooms of hydrangea, strawflowers, zinnias, globe amaranth, and roses into the artemisia. To add fullness, arrange and hot-glue individual stems of silk foliage and artemisia around the wreath and finish with a bow.

Designer: **Diane Weaver**

Brilliant Blossoms

$\mathcal{A}$ STORE-BOUGHT BASE OF GLYCERINE-PRESERVED PRINCESS pine provides a bright background for an assortment of colorful spring flowers. To make the wreath, first wire a paper bow to the base, then hot-glue dried blooms of zinneas, statice, roses, daffodils, caspia, baby's breath, and heather randomly into the pine. For greenery, hot-glue stems of eucalyptus and tree ferns.

Finish with a festive bow.

Designer:
Corinne Erb

Lady's-Mantle Wreath

*C*OLOR, ONE OF THE MOST IMPORTANT elements of any composition, is a striking feature of this vibrant wreath. This wreath is also testimony to the fact that dried flowers can be every bit as distinctive as their fresh counterparts.

To make the wreath, arrange small clusters of dried lady's-mantle and hot-glue them to a grapevine base, leaving room for a large bow. Next, attach several branches of sumac berries at various points around the wreath. Follow with stems of lavender and everlastings in shades of bone, burgundy, and purple. Tie a luxurious bow of metallic ribbon and glue it to the wreath so that its tendrils drape gracefully down either side.

Designer: **Jane Dicus**

Herbs for all Seasons

*T*HIS COLORFUL WREATH COMBINES PURPLE OREGANO FLOWERS with accents of a similar hue. To make the wreath, first cover a straw base with Spanish moss using floral pins. Then arrange stems of dried oregano blooms, dark red roses and leaves, pink and purple statice sinuata, baby's breath, German statice, and stock on floral picks and insert them into the base.

Designer:
Beth Stickle

Feathery Spray

A PERENNIAL HERB NATIVE TO EUROPE, tansy is welcomed in any garden, not for its historic culinary purposes but also for its usefulness as a dried flower. Its diminutive, bright yellow flowers stand on tall stems that are covered with fernlike leaves.

To make this feathery wreath, start with a crimped wire frame covered with moss. Cut 4-inch (10 cm) stems of peppergrass and secure them to the base with monofilament. Add texture with an assortment of other grasses glued on top. Finish the wreath with clusters of tansy buttons and single stems of yellow daisies hot-glued in place.

Designer: **Jeannette Hafner**

Zinnias!

ROAD, DAISYLIKE BLOSSOMS AND rounded doubles characterize zinnias, which bloom in a rainbow of colors. As cut flowers they often last for weeks, and when dried in silica gel, zinnias lose none of their vibrant color and maintain their full petal size and shape.

To make this bright, midsummer wreath, start with a wire ring base. Enlarge the base and give it some resilience by wrapping scrap pieces of artemisia all around, securing them in place with monofilament. Next, make small bundles of 4-inch (10 cm) pieces of artemisia and attach these around the base in a uniform spiral.

Tuck in pieces of lavender-grey caspia, and top the wreath with zinnias and pieces of purple larkspur. To prevent the fragile petals of the zinnias from breaking off, attach the flowers with a ring of hot glue dotted onto the backs of the petals. Add a navy satin bow for the finishing touch.

Designer: **Jeannette Hafner**

Sweetheart's Wreath

A SMALL, HEART-SHAPED GREENERY wreath purchased at a craft store was embellished with dried flowers and ribbon to create this very personal Valentine's Day statement. To make the wreath, fill in the greenery base with German statice and baby's breath, then hot-glue in blooms of celosia, globe amaranth, straw flowers, pepperberries, and a few roses for love. Add a narrow ribbon bow with long streamers for a finishing touch.

Designer: **Jeannette Hafner**

Yuletide Cheer

TRADITIONAL CHRISTMAS COLORS HIGHLIGHT THIS SMALL, EASY-to-make wreath that can be displayed as a wall or door decoration or placed around a candle as a table centerpiece. Start with a purchased base of artificial greenery and hot-glue short stems of dried German statice around the inner and outer edges of the greenery. Finish by hot-gluing small stems of pepperberries in the center.

Designer:
Jeannette Hafner

Impress Your Guests Wreath

*T*HIS STUNNING DRIED FLOWER WREATH makes a terrific first impression in your home. To make the wreath, cover a straw base with green oak leaves using greening pins. Next, cluster three to five stems of green sweet Annie in small bouquets and attach them to floral picks. Insert the picked bouquets into the base. Add bundles of Ti tree (dyed pink) and larkspur in the same manner. For a lacy finishing touch, fill in any bare spots with wispy stems of caspia.

Designer: **Julianne Bronder**

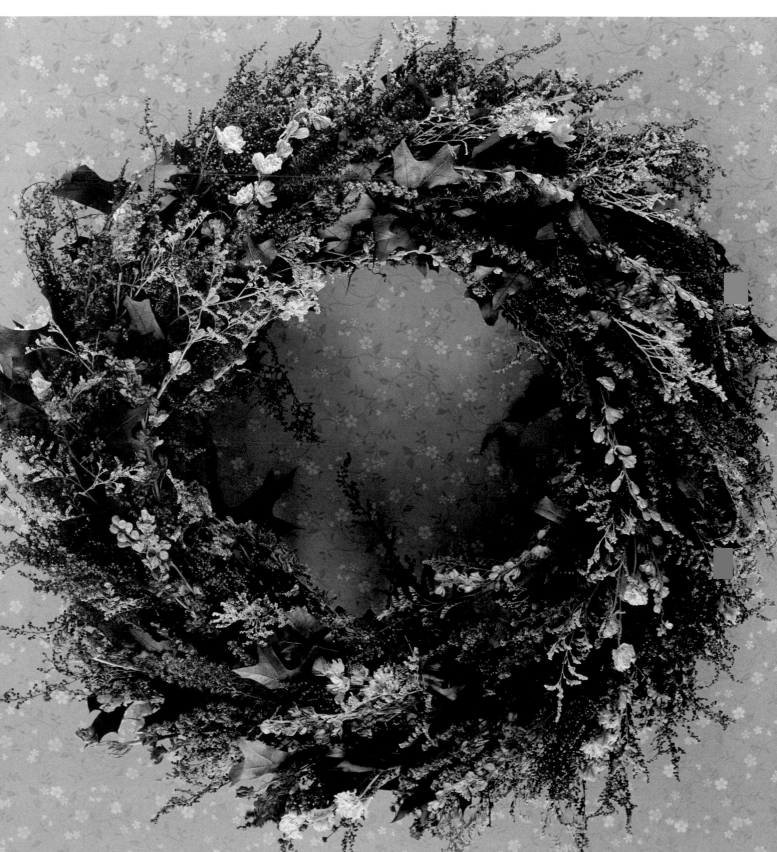

Showers of Flowers

$\mathcal{Y}$ELLOW BUTTONS OF SANTOLINA BLOOMS CONTRAST NICELY with slender spires of blue salvia. To make this wreath, wire stems of German statice onto a wire ring wreath base. Next, arrange stems of santolina, blue salvia, white strawflowers, annual statice, and mountain mint leaves onto floral picks, then hot-glue the picks into the German statice.

Designer:
Jane Dicus

Welcome Home Wreath

*B*UTTERY-YELLOW WALLS PROVIDE A sunny background for this cheerful and welcoming dried sunflower wreath. Start with a 10-inch (25 cm) straw wreath and reinforce it by wrapping with floral wire. Attach bracken ferns to floral picks and insert them into the base, positioning them so that the ferns angle out of the wreath instead of lying flat. Next, insert the larkspur in varying heights, following a spiral design. Pick in the sunflowers with the aim of creating loose, asymmetrical clusters. Then pick in the other dried flowers in this order: sandfordi, sweet Annie, rye, and lemon leaf. Use Spanish moss to cover any picks that may show.

Designer: **Josena Aiello McCaig**

Woodland Wreath

THIS WHITE-ON-WHITE DRIED FLOWER wreath with just a hint of color comes alive against the wallpaper in this friendly, sunny room. To make the wreath, cut a block of floral foam into two thin, rectangular pieces and press them into a 14-inch (36 cm) three-ring wire base. Trim away the excess foam and continue pressing the foam pieces into the base until it is completely filled. Cover the base with Spanish moss and secure it with thin-gauge floral wire. Next, insert stems of German statice around the outside of the entire wreath. Make bundles of white roses, wild baby's breath, silver-king artemisia, white yarrow, feverfew, boneset, oats, ammobium, lamb's ears, and fountain grass and attach the bundles to floral picks. Hot-glue in small blooms of strawflowers and blue salvia to provide contrast, then add an organdy ribbon.

Designer: **Cynthia Gillooly**

Unforgettable

*L*IKE BERRIES RIPE FOR THE PICKING, these deep magenta globes beckon the eye and the hand.

To make the wreath, first make a base by attaching short bunches of German statice to a wire ring with flo-ral tape. Overlap each bundle just enough to cover the stems of the preceding one. Next, place the amaranths together with small clusters of rue, white annual statice, and larkspur in shades of lavender and purple, hot-glu-ing them in place. Add a hint of greenery by hot-gluing in Mountain mint leaves.

Designer: **Jane Dicus**

Bunches of Berries Wreath

*C*ANELLA BERRIES, STRAWFLOWERS, wormwood, German statice, and small myrtle (branches and berries) create an enticing combination of color and texture in winter wreaths. To make the wreath, fill a double-wire ring base with silver-king artemisia. Attach small bouquets of the berries, strawflowers, and wormwood to flower picks and hot-glue their tips into the artemisia.

Designer: **Nancy McCauley**

Dainty Delight

*T*HE BOTANICAL NAME for the strawflowers featured in this wreath, *eranthemum*, derives from the Greek for "dry flower." The name is indicative of the papery texture of the dainty double flowers, which grow in a wide variety of colors. Its common name, immortelle, is equally fitting for a flower that dries so successfully. Because of its diminutive size, strawflowers are better suited to a small-scale wreath.

To make the wreath, start with a ring base evenly covered with miniature bouquets of German statice. (The statice makes an attractive background in the spaces between your more significant flowers.) To add the immortelle blossoms, touch each stem with a drop of hot glue, and insert it into the base. For a bit of contrast, add a few stems of dark blue larkspur and some individual mountain mint leaves in key locations around the wreath. For embellishment, attach a casual bow of fine satin ribbon.

Designer: **Jane Dicus**

Splendid Summer Wreath

A MELANGE OF PURPLE, RED, AND pink blooms creates this colorful harvest of summer color. To make the wreath, hot-glue short stems of preserved fern around a twig base. Next, hot-glue single blooms of strawflowers, roses, statice, zinnias, globe amaranth, and seed hyacinth to the twig base.

Designer: **Kim Tibbals Thompson**

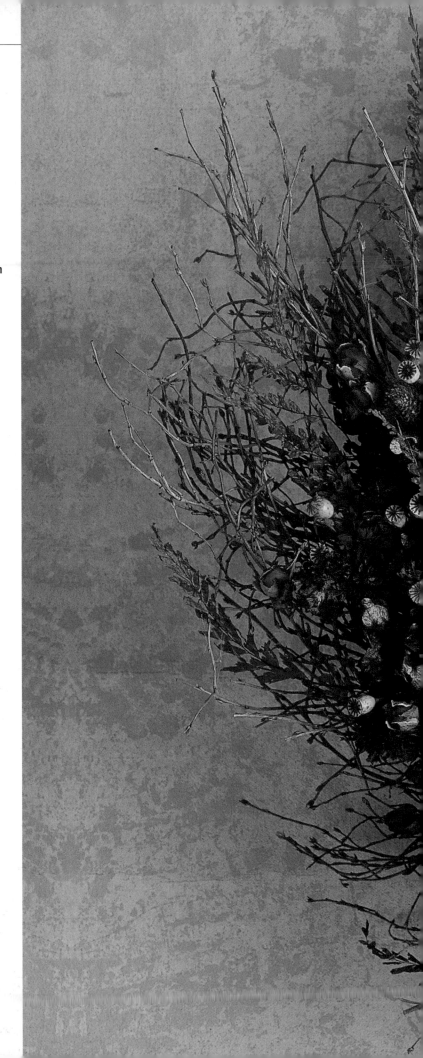

Lovely Lavender Wreath

*M*ANY OLD-FASHIONED PERENNIAL favorites also qualify as herbs, and lavender is a prime example. Noted for its gentle, clean fragrance, lavender has long been used for soaps, bath oil, and potpourri. A wreath made of fresh lavender can fill an entire room with scent. When dried, it holds nearly all its color and much of its fragrance.

To make this wreath, start with a small vine base. Cut several short lengths of brown yarn or fine-gauge wire to use for tying the flowers onto the vines. Then form bunches of caspia, placing about 20 to 30 lavender stems on the top of each bunch. Moving in a single direction around the base, tie or wire the bunches in a spiral pattern onto the wreath. Be sure to cover the stems and wire of each bunch with the flowers of the succeeding one. Using a narrow satin ribbon in a complementary shade of lavender, form loops, and hot-glue them randomly around the wreath.

Designer: **Alyce Nadeau**

Heavenly Hydrangea

*F*OR THOSE WHO HAVE A SHADY SITE, THERE are relatively few options when it comes to flowering shrubs. One of the finest is the hydrangea. This shrub not only tolerates low light but actually prefers it, and even a young plant will produce a generous number of enormous flower clusters. Its nonwhite varieties exhibit an unusual sensitivity to soil conditions: in a sweet soil, the blossoms are pink; blue flowers result from an acidic soil. As evidenced by this lush wreath, hydrangea maintains all of its glory when dried.

To make the wreath, cut small clusters of dried flowers, and assemble them onto picks. Begin on the inside circle of a straw wreath form and pick the flowers at an angle into the base. Make a second circle of flower clusters around the outside of the wreath. Then, using a zigzag pattern, fill in the top surface, angling and layering the clusters to fill out the wreath.

Add an accent ribbon by securing one cut end onto a pick, inserting it into the base, and looping and twining the ribbon. Finally, insert a small cluster of statice for a garnish.

Designer: **Clara Curtis**

Victorian Dreams

A VICTORIAN-INSPIRED COLOR SCHEME IS simple to create with dried flowers, and custom color combinations can be made to match your favorite table setting.

To make this wreath, attach small bouquets of dried German statice to floral picks, then cover a straw base with the statice. Next, loosely wrap a length of satin ribbon around the wreath, securing occasionally with dabs of hot glue. Fill out the wreath by hot-gluing in stems of tinted baby's breath, pepper grass, annual statice, and parchment paper flowers.

Designer: **Julianne Bronder**

Spread a Little Sunshine

A FAVORITE WITH CHILDREN AND ADULTS, sunflowers quickly grow to giant proportions, looming over the rest of the garden. And, as anyone who regularly feeds birds knows, they readily sprout from seeds. Some, like the blossoms used to make this cheerful wreath, are much more modest in scale. To make the wreath, begin by wiring short clusters of German statice onto a plastic or metal ring covered with floral tape. Note: Because German statice is very brittle and can be prickly to handle, you may wish to mist it with water and leave overnight before handling.) Next, hot-glue miniature sunflowers into prominent positions all around the wreath. To get a three-dimensional appearance, try to glue the flowers deep inside and outside the wreath, not just on the top. Add clusters of chinaberries, white annual statice, and stems of wheat.

Designer: **Jane Dicus**

Mother's Day Wreath

*S*PRING COLORS, RIBBONS, AND PEARLS LIGHT up this Mother's Day remembrance. To make the wreath, weave fresh-cut stems of purple hyacinth bean into a vine base. Next, hot-glue Mexican sage to the base, beginning at the top and working down each side. Then add strawflowers, globe amaranth, zinnias, and bee balm, and bells of Ireland to fill out the design. Hot-glue pearls to the center of each Bells of Ireland bloom, then glue two colors of narrow ribbon around the wreath.

Designer:
Diane Weaver

Anise Hyssop Beauty

*F*RAGRANT LAVENDER BLOOMS OF THIS little-known herb sway gracefully in the lightest breeze. Anise hyssop attracts honeybees and butterflies throughout the late summer months. It also attracts crafters. Hung upside down in an airy room, the purple blossoms dry well, retaining their shape and much of their color. To make the wreath, form mini bouquets of anise hyssop flowers and pick them into a grapevine base, leaving the top bare and adding extra fullness at the bottom. Include an occasional leaf as an accent. Finally, shape mini bouquets of Rose of Sharon blooms, and pick them in at strategic points.

Designer: **Nora Blose**

Great Shapes

LTHOUGH THE symbolic circular wreath shape has served us well for hundreds of years, there's no reason why a wreath can't be any shape you want it to be. If you're a traditionalist at heart, try experimenting with oval-shaped wreaths (see pages 93 and 95) or wreaths made from interlocking circles (see pages 105, 108, and 112). If you're a rebel at heart, turn straight to pages 90, 91, 97, and 101 for several spectacular square wreaths. And if you fall somewhere in between, the heart-shaped wreaths on pages 103, 152, and 153 should serve you well.

Unique

SMALL FLORAL SPRAYS AT OPPOSITE CORNERS accentuate the unique shape of this square wreath. To make the wreath, use floral pins to cover a square foam base with moss. Position four large silk leaves with their stems facing each other in one corner of the wreath, then hot-glue stems of dried larkspur, caspia, and dried roses over the leaves. Repeat the arrangement at the opposite corner, then weave loops of a narrow print ribbon throughout the wreath, hot-gluing as needed.

Designer: **Cynthia Gillooly**

Fit to Be Hung

*T*HIS SQUARE WREATH SHOWCASES BOTH herbal blooms and their stems. To make the wreath, start by making two galvanized-wire squares of different sizes. Center the smaller one (which will be the inside diameter) inside the larger one (for the outside diameter). Secure them with string-reinforced packing tape: wrap the tape around the two squares, forming two "bridges" of tape, one at top and one at bottom

Wrap sphagnum moss around the base—both wires and the webbing—to form a square base with a hole in the middle. Cut basil stems to the right length and lay them on the base. Run a piece of wire over them at top and bottom, and attach the wire ends to the back of the base. Wrap pieces of thyme around the basil wood.

To finish, hot-glue on the remaining materials: lamb's ear, poppy seedheads, bells of Ireland, thistle leaves, globe amaranth, zinnia, tansy, pearly everlasing, dusty miller leaves, silver germander, and allium flowers. Wire on a raffia braid for a hanger, and glue a few flowers to it.

Designer:

Diane Weaver

Twisted Twig Wreath

WITH ITS MILK-WASHED TWIG BASE, organdy bow, and sprinkling of pansies, this dried flower wreath is as delicate and fresh as spring.

To make the wreath, spray a base with white wash floral spray. Next, create the background of the wreath by hot-gluing clusters of dried lady's-mantle, sweet Annie, mugwort, and yarrow to the base, leaving space at the top for the bow. Next, glue on bundles of pearly everlasting, ammobium, and feverfew. Divide the wreath into thirds with pink cockscomb. Add pink globe amaranth, dispersing it around the wreath so that pink is the predominant color. As a final blessing, glue on the fragile pansies and organdy bow.

Designer. **Barbara Applebaum**

Un-Ordinary Oval

*O*VAL-SHAPED BASES ALLOW CRAFTERS TO create wreaths with interior design considerations in mind. (Vertically positioned ovals look especially nice on doors, while horizontals work well on long walls.) To make the wreath, attach small bouquets of sweet Annie and preserved fern to floral picks, then hot-glue the picks into an oval wreath base. Arrange a long length of French ribbon into a bow with curved streamers and hot-glue it to the center top of the wreath. Finish by hot-gluing single blooms and stems of strawflowers, dahlias, zinnias, beebalm, love-in-a-mist, salvia Victoria, Mexican bush sage, and assorted pods into the sweet Annie.

Designer: **Diane Weaver**

Pendulum

A HANGING BOW AND ribbon streamer creates a unique shape for this dried flower wall display. To make the wreath, attach a paper bow to the center top of a moss base. Hot-glue stems of pussy willow, German statice, and silk blooms under and around the bow. Make a second bow with long streamers and attach it to the back of the wreath with floral pins, then decorate the top bow with a single bloom and German statice.

Designer:
Julianne Bronder

A Natural Beauty

*O*VAL-SHAPED WREATHS LOOK ESPECIALLY NICE WITH varying degrees of fullness, as in this herbal wreath made from fresh lady's-mantle. (If you don't happen to have a garden full of blooming lady's-mantle, just substitute your favorite feathery bloom.) To make the wreath, attach stems of lady's mantle to floral picks and insert them into a vine base. Attach a bow at top, allowing the streamers to float down over the flowers.

Designer:

Nora Blose

Fancy Frame

A FILIGREE OF BENT TWIGS FORMS A square base for an off-center spray of fernlike foliage and artificial fruit. To make the wreath, hot-glue a few tips of preserved plumosa, followed by a stem or two of artificial bean pods with foliage onto the lower right corner of a square twig base. Add a cluster of artificial pomegranates and a loose raffia bow.

At the top, wind a long stem of bean pods and foliage through the lacy frame, and hot-glue it in place. Add one last stem of plumosa and a feathered bird to complete the arrangement.

Designer: **Cynthia Gillooly**

Pretty as a Picture

$\mathcal{H}$ERE'S ANOTHER SQUARE WREATH WITH enough charm to challenge any circular competition. To make the wreath shown, bend galvanized wire into a square and tape the ends together. Also make a wire circle small enough to fit well inside the square. These will form the outer and inner bases of the wreath. Wire bunches of dried marjoram onto the square, and wire globe thistles to the circle. Then wire the circle on top of the square base. Hot-glue the accents to the base: boneset, curry flowers, globe amaranth, yarrow, bee balm, and mint.

Designer: **Diane Weaver**

Berry Simple Bow

𝒯HE CAREFREE NATURE OF DRIED BITTERSWEET CREATES
this whimsical wreath shape. To make the wreath, weave branches
of fresh-cut bittersweet in between the layers of a grapevine wreath base,
securing with dabs of hot glue as needed. Add a large paper bow to finish.

Designer:
Gail Martin

Laticework Wreath

*T*HIS GORGEOUS ARTIFICIAL WREATH perfectly complements the fabric in the armchair, while the lattice base echoes the stenciled woodwork in the glass door.

Start by wiring ivy to the inner edge of the vine base and cover the wire with small clumps of moss. Wire on large silk tulips and large and small mums. Next, wire on the berry clusters. Glue or wire on clusters of miniature roses and greenery. Finish the wreath with a very light dusting of ferns and baby's breath.

Designer: **Julianne Bronder**

Rock-a-Bye Wreath

*L*OVE-IN-A-MIST IS PRIZED BY FLORAL designers for its papery seed pods. With their broad burgundy stripes against a pale green background, the pods make dramatic accents in all manner of floral arrangements.

To make this wreath, first tie a clump of raffia into a knot at the top. Using a few extra strands of raffia, clasp the base together at several points, then clip off any loose ends at the knots. Wire a well-soaked bouquet holder onto the bottom of the base, and insert stems of lavender and pink silk flowers along with a few galax leaves and stems of variegated ivy. Tuck in small clumps of moss as needed.

Designer: **Tommy Wallen**

Hip to Be Square

*T*HIS ELABORATE WREATH IS A MAJOR UNDER-taking, but the results are spectacular. To create the base, first draw a pattern on a piece of paper, glue it to a two-inch-thick (5 cm) sheet of rigid foam, and cut out the base with a sharp knife. After you've got the basic shape, use the knife to sculpt various levels. Then hot-glue on the materials, starting at the top and working downward, overlapping the leaves and petals in the same direction.

Green eucalyptus leaves define the contours of the wreath. Other materials include feverfew, tansy (note the individual flowers glued on the upper inside curves), rose petals, larkspur, zinnia, blue and white salvia, lamb's ear, globe amaranth, Mexican sage, starflowers, and hydrangea seedpods.

Designer: **Diane Weaver**

Be My Valentine

*L*ARGE STEMS OF HYDRANGEA BLOOMS make an ideal filler material for large, lush wreaths.

To make this wreath, hot-glue a large bow and curving streamers to the center top of a heart-shaped peppergrass wreath base. Separate the hydrangea clusters into smaller sections and hot-glue them around the top and sides of the base. Finish by hot-gluing stems and single blooms of larkspur, carnations, roses, strawflowers, common immortelle, love-in-a-mist, and lemon leaves.

Designer: **Kim Tibbals Thompson**

Display Wreath

*E*MBELLISH YOUR FAVORITE framed paintings and photographs with small wreaths, custom-coordinated to match your home's decor. To make the wreath, begin by wrapping a small foam base with ribbon, securing on the back side with sewing pins. Hot-glue an arrangement of dried roses, strawflowers, and yarrow at the top of the wreath.

To hang the wreath, hot-glue one end of a length of wide ribbon to each side of the back of a photo frame. Bring the remaining ribbons together and hot-glue them to the back of the wreath base. Reinforce the ribbons with a floral pin.

Designer: **Fred Gaylor**

Two of a Kind

ENTWINED OVAL BASES CREATE A UNIQUE wreath base that's fun to decorate and display. To make the wreath, first secure two oval grapevine bases together with heavy-gauge wire. Weave a length of wired ribbon through each base, starting at the bottom and working your way up and around, securing with hot glue as needed. When you reach the top of each base, wrap the ribbon length under the vine. Bring the ribbons together at their ends and secure with wire, then cover the wire with a short length of ribbon. Decorate the wreath by hot-gluing stems of silk berries, silk flowers, and fresh-cut yarrow into the vine.

Designer: **Cynthia Gillooly**

Spiral Splendor

A DELICATE PALETTE OF PASTEL COLORS decorates this simple and elegant paper ribbon wreath. To make the wreath, curl twisted paper ribbon in loop shapes and secure with floral-tape-covered wire. On a flat surface, fashion a spray from the lilacs, roses, and heather, and wire them together. Then wire the spray to the upper tier of paper ribbon loops. Secure a second, smaller cluster of flowers, and wire it to form the lower bouquet.

Designer: **Julianne Bronder**

Whimsy

SCARLET BEE BALM flowers dress up a base made of another interesting herb: broom. The leggy, yellow-green foliage was at one time tied into bundles and used to sweep the floor, not adorn the wall. To make the wreath, form a sheaf of broom into a circle, and tape it together with floral tape, then hotglue bee balm flowers over the taped areas.

Designer: **Nora Blose**

Thrice as Nice

HIS TRIPLE WREATH IS THE PERFECT backdrop to show off the two most common colors of larkspur. To make the base, lay three wire rings together so that the center one is on top, and tape them together with duct tape or packing tape. Then weave whole stems of larkspur around the circles, staggering them so that all portions of the circles have some blossoms. Hot-glue more larkspur flowers onto the base, filling all the holes, until the base is as full as you want it. Glue on the remaining materials: globe amaranth, zinnias, strawflowers, cockscomb, and lamb's ear. Finally, wire on the bow.

Designer: **Diane Weaver**

The Birdhouse

A FLOWER AS UNUSUAL AS THE BIRD-OF-paradise deserves a setting equally unconventional. To make this dramatic wreath, hot-glue melaleuca bark onto a pentagonal foam base. Wire a bouquet holder to the base and insert the birds-of-paradise and a few miniature schefflera leaves and clusters of golden asters into the bouquet holder. Hot-glue a few stems of curly willow and wire a lichen-covered branch to the base. Finish by hot-gluing small pieces of moss around the wreath to hire any pieces of wire or the bouquet holder.

Designer: **Janet Frye**

Catmint and Vine

A CLOSE RELATIVE OF CATNIP, CATMINT IS less prone to send the neighborhood felines into flights of ecstasy and it makes a great material for wreaths.

To make this simple wreath, twist several small vines into a circle and wire them together at the bottom. Form two full bouquets of fresh catmint, and wire them to the base, with the stems in the center and the spiky blooms pointing to the outside. Add a bow made with two strips of narrow ribbon, one lavender and one green.

Designer: **Nora Blose**

Trio

*T*HIS TRIPLE WREATH IS THE perfect shape for a tall, thin wall space. To make the wreath, wire and hot-glue three twig wreaths together. Add bows where the wreaths connect and at the top. Next, arrange and hot-glue stems of silk greenery and blooms around the wreaths. Finish by wiring faux birds in place.

Designer:
Julianne Bronder

Wedding Bands

WHAT IMAGE COULD BETTER EXPRESS THE essence of matrimony than two rings, like two lives or spirits, linked and growing together? This dainty double wreath captures the feeling perfectly with red roses for love and pink roses for romance on a natural background suggestive of bridal lace. To make the wreath, first form the double base by taping together two rings of heavy galvanized (clothes line) wire and covering the wire with wired-on clumps of Spanish moss. Next, attach bunches of silver king artemisia to the bases, starting at the top and working along each ring in one direction from the outside to the inside. Finish by hot-gluing dried roses, strawflowers, baby's breath, hyacinth, dusty miller, and globe amaranth around the rings, concentrating them at the top.

Designer: **Diane Weaver**

Evergreens & Greenery

A STAPLE OF THE traditional Christmas wreath, evergreens have been used in holiday celebrations since the days of ancient Rome. Sturdy enough to last through the holiday season, many types of evergreens have the added benefit of emitting those wonderful fragrances we love to bring into our homes in the winter. Varieties of pine, holly, hemlock, cedar, boxwood, and ivy are popular choices for wreath making, but don't overlook other types of greenery such as ferns, herbs, and your favorite shrubs. Evergreens and greenery can be preserved with a glycerin treatment (see page 31), attached to a base in water-filled floral tubes, or attached to a wreath when fresh cut and left to dry naturally in place.

Sweet Scent Potpourri Wreath

A SMALL BAG OF STORE-BOUGHT potpourri adds color and strawberry fragrance to this bright holiday wreath. To make the wreath, spread a thick layer of craft glue around three-fourths of small foam base base. Press the potpourri into the glue and allow it to completely to dry.

Attach stems of silk apples, roses, cranberries, and branches of glycerin-preserved to floral picks and arrange them on the bare portion of the base.

Designer: **Fred Gaylor**

Garden Treasures

*I*NSTEAD OF ARRANGING YOUR GARDEN treasures in the typical vase, arrange them around a wreath for a stunning display. To make the wreath, soak a small oasis foam base in water. Attach stems of berries, privet, dusty miller, and wandering Jew to floral picks and insert them into the base. Fill in the gaps with small clumps of moss. To use as a centerpiece, place the wreath on a plate or platter and put a large candle in the center.

Designer: **Fred Gaylor**

Myrtle and Yew Fruit Bowl

A LIVING CENTERPIECE WREATH IS MUCH more fun to water than your average house plant. To make the wreath, soak an oasis wreath base in water. Dip the stems of fresh-cut myrtle and wandering Jew (or other plants that root easily) in rooting hormone and insert them into the base. Place the wreath on a serving platter and place a fruit bowl in the center.

Designer: **Fred Gaylor**

Simple Oak Leaf Wreath

*P*INE BOUGHS AND HOLLY AREN'T THE ONLY way to create the deep green background so popular and attractive in natural Christmas decorations. This lush wreath uses preserved oak leaves (available through craft or floral dealers) to achieve the same effect with a softer texture and a more bushy fullness. To make the wreath, hot-glue a generous quantity of leaves around a grapevine base, then add cane coils (another natural, craft-store item) and a bow.

Designer: **Julianne Bronder**

Potted Wreath

A LIVING TOPIARY WREATH IS EASY TO CREATE when you use a cooperative plant such as rosemary or ivy.

To make this wreath, first insert a sturdy metal or wood rod into a pot of dirt. Attach a wire ring base onto the top of the rod with electrical tape. Weave long lengths of fresh-cut ivy around the wire ring and mist well with water. Care for and display the topiary wreath as you would any house plant.

Designer: **Fred Gaylor**

A Classic Christmas

PINES, RED BOWS, AND BERRIES ARE probably the most common components of Christmas wreaths, but a truly amazing variety of unique designs can be created from this familiar trio. To make this wreath, wire a large bow onto a store-bought base of dried baby's breath. Next, hot-glue in small stems of pine. Attach clusters of silk berries to floral picks and hot-glue them into the base.

Designer: **Julianne Bronder**

Simple Wreath

THIS HANDSOME WREATH CONTRASTS wonderfully with most natural woods, making it an ideal wall piece for paneled or heavily wooded rooms. To make the wreath, attach bundles of preserved fern and sweet Annie to floral picks and then hot-glue the picks into a vine wreath base. Add color to the background by hot-gluing carnations, globe amaranth, sago, larkspur, Mexican sage, and agapanthus into the background materials.

Designer: **Diane Weaver**

Menagerie

WHILE EVERGREENS PROVIDE THE enticing fragrance of this wreath, flowers and herbs from a summer garden provide the bright, cheerful colors.

To make the wreath, attach handfuls of balsam branches to a straw base with floral pins. Loop a length of green ribbon around the wreath, securing it with hot glue every few inches (8 cm). To finish, hot-glue stems of dried flowers, greenery, and spices into the balsam. Roses, carnations, caspia, sweet Annie, statice, zinnias, eucalyptus, lamb's ear, pussy willows, strawflowers, cockscomb, artemisia, boxwood, Princess pine, tree ferns, nutmeg, and star anise were used in this wreath. After a few weeks, the fresh balsam will dry naturally on the wreath and its wonderful fragrance will remain.

Designer: **Corinne Erb**

Fabulously Fragrant

FRESH EVERGREEN WREATHS CAN BE A DELIGHT FOR THE nose as well as the eye, filling your home with the cheery scent of a pine forest. To make this wreath, start by hot-gluing sprays of blueberry cedar around a grapevine base. Next, pick stems of dried blue salvia into the cedar. Add small clumps of reindeer moss around the wreath.

Designer: **Julianne Bronder**

Marvelous Miscellany

*U*NCONVENTIONAL MATERIALS ARRANGED in the most traditional fashion can result in a stunning wreath.

Here the "background" material consists of two varieties of cypress shrub, one a silvery blue and the other a deep, forest green. These are complemented by sprigs of two broad-leafed evergreens: andromeda and holly. Soft, silvery pussy willow grouped with dark, spiky seed heads from black-eyed Susans, golden paulownia berries, and pale pink heather create a harmony of colors and textures. A branch of Siberian iris pods completes the assortment. The construction couldn't be simpler; just attach stems of the materials onto floral picks and pick them into a straw base in a spiral pattern.

Designer: **Sandy Mush Herb Nursery**

Scent of the Season

AMAZINGLY, IT TAKES ONLY A FEW branches of fraser fir to emit the wonderful fragrance of Christmas. To make the wreath, begin by picking stems of dried German statice and fresh fraser fir into a straw base. Next, create a spray of dried feverfew, sumac, strawflowers, bay leaves, ivy, sweet Annie, silver king artemisia, fraser fir, and German statice at the bottom of the wreath by picking the materials into the base.

Designer: **Sandy Mush Herb Nursery**

Handsome Holiday Wreath

ELEBRATE THE HOLIDAYS WITH A WREATH that's bursting with fragrance, color, and texture. To make the wreath, attach stems of fraser fir to floral picks and insert them around the outer and inner edges of a straw wreath base. Next, insert picked stems of canella berries, German statice, gypsophilia, dyed yarrow, dusty miller, pearly everlasting, pine cones, and seed heads into the base. Fill any gaps with small clumps of moss.

Designer: **Nancy McCauley**

Reflections

A FOAM WREATH BASE WITH A mirrored center reflects the natural beauty of fresh flowers. To make the wreath, cut a small piece of wet floral foam and hot-glue it to the bottom of the wreath base. Insert fresh-cut flowers and greenery into the foam (carnations and galax leaves were used here). Next, attach stems of silk greenery, berries, and evergreens to floral picks and insert them into the base. Finish by hot-gluing small tree ornaments, pussy willow branches, and ribbon streamers around the wreath.

Designer: **Aubrey Gibson**
and Michael Staley

Holly, Berries, and a Big Bow

*T*HE SIMPLEST MATERIALS—FRESH HOLLY and berries—often create the most beautiful wreaths. To make this wreath, attach fresh-cut stems of holly on floral picks and insert them into a moss-covered straw base. Arrange stems of fresh-cut green berries on a sheet of newspaper outdoors and give them a light spray of red paint. (Do not overspray: Some of the berries' green color should show through the red.) Finish with a large, multi-looped bow.

Designer: **Fred Gaylor**

A Labor of Love

ONE COULD ALMOST IMAGINE A RUNNER of ivy growing naturally to form this lovely Valentine wreath. The secret to its airy design is the hand-crafted wire base. To make the base, cut six lengths of 18-gauge wire to 18 inches (45 cm). Holding three pieces of wire together, bend them into half of a heart shape. Repeat with the remaining three pieces of wire, then secure the two sides together with floral tape. Next, loosely wrap stems of silk ivy around the base, then follow with three colors of thin satin ribbon, securing as needed with hot glue. Finish by hot-gluing German statice, straw flowers, celosia, roses, and globe amaranth into the ivy.

Designer: **Janet Frye**

Eye-Catching

ℋ OLLY BERRIES, STAR ANISE, FRESH boxwood, fresh cedar, bay leaves, and mosses make a stunning wreath when creatively arranged.

To make the wreath, hot-glue three rows of individual bay leaves into a fresh evergreen base. Next, hot-glue short stems of holly berries on the center surface, then hot-glue star anise on top of and around the berries. Finish with small clumps of moss and a red ribbon bow.

Designer: **Corinne Erb**

Fountain Wreath

THE WATER MIST FROM A TABLETOP fountain helps keep the living ivy in this wreath fresh and moist. To make the wreath, soak an oasis form in water and wrap it with green foil ribbon. Wrap long stems of ivy around the wreath until most of the base is invisible. Place the wreath on a large platter or plate and place the fountain in the center.

Designer: **Fred Gaylor**

Lush, Plush Protea Wreath

LARGE GLYCERIN-PRESERVED PROTEA LEAVES form exotic curves when used as a background material. To make the wreath, attach small clusters of the protea leaves to floral picks and insert them into a straw base. Next, attach small bouquets of dried baby's breath that has been tinted a pale green to floral picks and insert them in between the leaves. (Note: If you can't find dyed baby's breath, just spritz the dried blooms with a light misting of water and food coloring.)

Designer: **Julianne Bronder**

Majestic Magnolias

MAGNOLIA LEAVES AND SEED PODS MAKE a stunning display on a large door wreath. To make the wreath, start by attaching magnolia leaves to floral picks. Starting at the center top of the wreath, insert the leaves down each side of a large straw base with their stems facing the center point, overlapping to create a solid texture of leaves. Place the seed pods around the wreath and attach under leaves with hot glue.

To create the top arrangement, make a fan of leaves in a flower shape at the center top of the wreath. Cut ribbon streamers from red velvet and glue them under the leaves. Finish with a large red bow.

Designer: **Fred Gaylor**

Dogwood Blossom Special

*T*HE MAGNOLIA LEAVES COVERING THIS wreath form a striking background for delicate blossoms of pink dogwood. To make the wreath, attach stems of glycerine-preserved magnolia leaves to floral picks and insert them into a straw base. (Note: Getting the leaves to lie flat while curving them around the base may take some extra time and maneuvering.) Next, wire a bow to one side of the wreath and hot-glue small sprigs of dried baby's breath into the bow's loops. Pick the silk dogwood blooms into the base between the leaves.

Designer: **Julianne Bronder**

Boxwood Beauty

*L*IGHT UP YOUR WINTER SEASON WITH A candle-lit boxwood wreath.

To make the wreath, start by working an indentation with a butter knife in the bottom center of a straw base. Keep working the straw until the indentation is large enough to insert the bottom of a battery-operated candle light. Squirt hot glue in the hole and press the candle in place. Next, attach stems of fresh-cut boxwood to floral picks and insert them around the outer, inner, and center surfaces of the base. Add a large red bow and enjoy.

Designer: **Fred Gaylor**

Sweet Cinnamon

FOAM BASES COVERED WITH CRUSHED cinnamon are just one of the many innovative types of bases being marketed by wreath manufacturers. The cinnamon fragrance in this base is very strong when first purchased, and can be rejuvenated with a few drops of cinnamon oil as time passes and the scent fades.

To make this wreath, create the top arrangement by attaching a large cotton bow with floral wire and then picking in stems of silk pine under the bow's loops. Next, hot-glue several cinnamon sticks, then fill out the spray with stems of dried pepper-grass, German statice, and annual statice.

Create the bottom arrangement with the same materials, using a pine cone and a spray of berries as the focal point instead of another bow.

Designer:
Julianna Diondei

Bounteous Bay Leaf Wreath

*L*ARGE, LUSH, AND FULL, THIS WREATH STILL looks light enough to hang above a delicate mantle. To make the wreath, begin by wiring small clus-ters of fresh bay leaf branches wire ring base. Next, attach gold sleigh bells to the base with wire, then hot-glue zinnias, boneset, strawflowers, artemisia, and pink berries into the bay leaves.

Designer: **Diane Weaver**

Holidays & Special Occasions

WHAT'S A CELEBRATION without decorations? And what decorates better than a festive wreath? Whether it's a centerpiece table wreath for a dinner party, a wedding wreath to decorate the church door, a seasonal wreath to mark passing time, or a festive display of holiday spirit that welcomes everyone who comes to your door, wreaths are an easy and fun way to celebrate any special occasion. Although you'll find many traditional wreath favorites in this chapter (evergreen Christmas wreaths with large red bows and harvest wreaths with bounties of fruits and nuts, for instance), you'll also find a wonderful variety of wreaths for special occasions year 'round. Just about anything can be celebrated with a wreath, so check your calendar now for upcoming occasions.

Advent Candles Wreath

*T*HE FOUR SUNDAYS BEFORE CHRISTMAS mark the season of Advent, a time of joyous preparation. What better way to get ready for the coming holiday than to set your table around an Advent wreath displaying a candle for each week of the season.

To make this wreath, begin by wrapping artificial greenery around and through a wire base. Hot-glue baby's breath, silk flowers, grape clusters, and small bouquets of Russian sage and salvia. Next, drape a length of ribbon around the surface and nestle a circular brass candle holder in the center.

Designer: **Nora Blose**

Festive Centerpiece

*V*IRTUALLY ANY WALL WREATH CAN BE displayed on a table as a centerpiece, and the center hole makes a convenient place for a large candle.

To make this wreath, pick small bouquets of German statice into a straw wreath base, then hot-glue coneflowers, zinnias, strawflowers, globe amaranth, love-in-a-mist, feverfew, and chamomile into the statice.

Designer: **Dolly Lutz Morris**

Antique-Look Easter Wreath

*S*OFT COLORS, LACY RIBBON, AND A STUFFED depression doll rabbit give an antique, country flavor to this Easter wreath. To make the wreath, wrap a grapevine base at intervals with antique lace ribbon. Cover the ends with a large bow. Next, insert parchment paper leaves into the vines, then add silk flowers and berries with hot glue. Attach the rabbit to the base with wire.

Designers:
Nora Blose and Michelle West

Just Right for Baby

*S*OFT AND WOOLY DRIED PAMPAS GRASS GIVES this wreath the feel of a cuddly warm blanket, making it an ideal gift to celebrate a new addition to the family. And long afterwards, the stuffed animal will remind the parents (and someday the child) of your thoughtfulness. To make the wreath, weave stems of pampas grass into a grapevine base, then wire the stuffed animal and the bow in place. To finish, hot-glue stems of zinnias, swamp sunflowers, German statice, and delphinium into the pampas grass.

Designer: **Diane Weaver**

Say It With Flowers

*F*LOWERS HAVE LONG BEEN GIVEN MEANINGS apart from their loveliness, and no culture has ever used that hidden language more effectively and eloquently than the Victorians. A heart-shaped wreath graced with appropriate herbs and flowers speaks of love in its beauty and its meaning.

For this wreath, begin with a heart-shaped wire frame. Wrap the frame with scraps of artemisia stems to give it bulk, and secure them in place with monofila-ment spiralled around several times. Again using monofilament, attach short stems of artemisia blossoms around the base. Finally, hot-glue the decorative flowers onto the artemisia, starting at the top and ending at the base, matching the flowers on either side. This wreath includes blue salvia (I think of you), carnations (bonds of affection), celosia (affection), globe amaranth (immortality), lavender (devotion), marjoram (joy and happiness), nigella (love-in-a-mist), roses (love), rosemary (remembrance) and thyme (courage).

Designer: **Jeannette Hafner**

Dazzle Your Darling

S MALL, HEART-SHAPED WREATHS CAN BE created inexpensively from vine bases and garden flowers, and make memorable alternatives to greeting cards on special occasions.

To make the wreath, hot-glue lemon tree leaves around the outside edge of the base, then cover the remaining surface area with larkspur, daisies, globe amaranth, baby everlastings, roses, daffodils, and baby's breath.

Designer: **Diane Weaver**

Lovebirds

*Y*OU CAN ALMOST HEAR THE LOVE BIRDS cooing on this frilly white wedding wreath that combines matrimonial symbolism with bridal accessories.

To make the wreath, first cover a heart-shaped straw base with white paper ribbon, then a layer of glitzy opalescent ribbon, and finally with a loose layer of white lace. Fasten a bridal veil to the top of the wreath and a garter to the bottom with corsage pins. Finish by hot-gluing the doves, a bow, and a strand of pearls to the base.

Designer: **Michelle West**

For the Wedding

*T*HIS CHARMING WEDDING WREATH WAS designed to hang on the outside of the church door during the ceremony; after the ceremony, remove the bird seed bags and give them to guests for the reception festivities.

To make the wreath, wrap a foam base with white moire ribbon, securing it on the back side as needed with pins. Wire a large bow to the top of the wreath. Pin silk greenery and flowers around each side of the bow and hot-glue small pieces of fern around the silk ivy.

To make the bird seed bags, place a spoon of bird seed in the center of a rectangular piece of tulle. Bring the edges up around the bird seed and tie with white ribbon. Attach the bags to the wreath base with dress-maker pins, then hot-glue a small satin rosebud to some of the bags for an extra touch.

Designer: **Julianne Bronder**

Wearable Wreath

*I*N LATIN, "CORONA" MEANS BOTH WREATH and crown. And what could be more appropriate for the bride than a crown of flowers and ribbons.

To make this wearable wreath, measure a length of heavy-gauge wire to fit around the intended wearer's head. Add 3 inches (7.5 cm) to that measurement and cut the wire. Form a 10-inch (2.5 cm) loop on one end of the wire. Place the wire vertically on your working surface so that the loop is in front of you. Next, hold 2-inch (5 cm) stems of baby's breath and strawflowers against the wire with their stems facing up and secure them to the wire with green floral tape.

Continue adding blooms until you've covered all but 2 inches of the wire. To wear, curve the wire to fit your head and form a hook to attach to the loop with the excess wire. Tie on silk ribbon streamers if desired.

Designer: **Gail Martin**

Miniatures

MINIATURE WREATH BASES MAKE AN ATTRACTIVE form for napkin rings and are easy to decorate. To make these napkin rings, loosely wrap a length of pearls or thin satin ribbon around small silk greenery bases, hot-gluing intermittently as needed. Create a small arrangement from small sprigs and blooms and hot-glue them in place. Finish with a small bow if desired.

Designer: **Dolly Lutz Morris**

Twinkling Wreath

TINY TWINKLING CHRISTMAS LIGHTS AND lacy bags of fragrant potpourri make this wreath a treat for the senses, especially in a darkened room. To make the wreath, work a string of lights into a long silk garland, then work the garland around a wire base.

Make small sachets by placing a spoon full of potpourri in the middle of a square of pink tulle. Gather the tulle up over the potpourri and tie with ribbon. Hot-glue the sachets into the greenery, then hot-glue small clusters of dried or silk hydrangea around the wreath. Finish with a festive bow with long streamers woven around the wreath.

Designers: **Nora Blose and Michelle West**

Touched by an Angel

ARTIFICIAL FRUITS AND SPRUCE BRANCHES in shades of blue, teal, and green create the look of a verdigris finish in this wreath.

To make the wreath, attach stems of silk spruce to floral picks and insert them into a straw base. Reinforce with hot glue if needed. Next, hot-glue a paper-mache angel into the spruce and add silk fruits and berries around the wreath. Last, hot-glue pinecones and a bow of metallic cord to the base. Note: If you can't find silk fruits with gold tones, just add gold highlights by giving them a light spray of gold paint.

Designer: **Fred Gaylor**

Floral Napkin Rings

WITH ONLY A MODICUM OF EFFORT AND materials, you can make a matching set of napkin rings and candle holders that will impress even the most discriminating guest. For the napkin rings, decorate each a little differently, using a glue gun to attach silk flowers, miniature greenery, and dried grasses. Don't go overboard with your decorations; it's much easier to insert the napkins into the rings if you leave much of the vine base exposed.

Designer: **Julianne Bronder**

Classy Candle Rings

*F*OR MATCHING CANDLE RINGS, BUILD TWO vine bases that are both about six inches (15 cm) in outside diameter. Then, with your glue gun, add the same or similar flowers that you used for the napkin rings on the facing page. This pair includes some German statice and a few bay leaves in addition to silk flowers, greenery, and dried grasses. When decorating your candle rings, arrange your flowers and greens at varying levels to result in greater depth and visual interest.

Designer: **Julianne Bronder**

Baby's First Wreath

THE ADORABLE TEDDY BEARS IN THIS wreath will keep a baby company for many months to come. To make the wreath, wrap a straw base with satin ribbon, then wrap over the ribbon with white tulle. Allow some extra tulle to trail downward at the bottom of the wreath. Attach the bears to the wreath with wire and attach the letters around the wreath with hot glue. Create a floral spray around the bears by hot-gluing stems of silk flowers and dried baby's breath around the bears. Finish by hot-gluing baby rattles and ribbon loops in place.

Designer: **Tommy Wallen**

Child's Wreath

*T*HIS SIMPLE WREATH WILL BRING YEARS OF pleasure to a child's room, yet is simple enough to make in an hour.

To make the wreath, first tie a teddy bear into a silk greenery base. Hot-glue peach and red bows and ribbon streamers around the wreath, then weave a length of lace around the wreath and hot-glue more bows to the lace. Finish by hot-gluing silk rosebuds around the wreath.

Designer: **Nicole Victoria**

Sophistication

$\mathcal{P}$ALE MAUVE AND SLATE BLUE ARE NOT THE first colors that spring to mind when we think of Christmas, but the tasteful use of these hues makes this elegant Yuletide wreath an ideal decoration for rooms where bold statements in red and green might seem

out of place. To make the wreath, first weave a blue velvet ribbon and a garland of pearl beads through a silk evergreen wreath, securing with hot glue where necessary. Next, hot-glue mauve silk peony blooms, small glass tree ornaments, and small pine cones around the wreath. Finish by hot-gluing or wiring a favorite tree ornament to the bottom of the wreath.

Designers:

Aubrey Gibson,
Alecia Godfrey,
and Beth Welch

Affectionately Yours

*S*ENDING MESSAGES OF AFFECTION expressed through the language of flowers is a tradition that has thrived since the Victorian Age. This dainty heart-shaped wreath delivers its missive with delicate dried materials and potpourri. To make the wreath, first coat the top and sides of a foam base with craft glue and press green potpourri into the surface. Let the glue completely dry, then hot-glue on the flowers. This wreath uses white daisies for innocence, hibiscus for delicate beauty, mint for virtue, fern for sincerity, pansies to say, "You occupy my thoughts," and red salvia to cover any bare spots.

Designer: **Dawn Cusick**

Gumdrop Wreath

*H*ERE'S A QUICK AND EASY TABLE WREATH to highlight a luncheon buffet, an hors d'oeuvre spread for a baby shower, a child's party, or even an Easter gathering.

Shown here with a candle, this wreath could also encircle a bowl of snacks, dip, or mints. To make the wreath, attach candy gumdrops to a foam wreath base with halved toothpicks.

Designers: **Aubrey Gibson, Alecia Godfrey, and Beth Welch**

great success. To make a wreath ornament, thread a piece of floral wire though a piece of lace 15 inches (37.5 cm) long and 4 inches (10 cm) wide, gathering it by going in and out of the holes until you've formed a 7-inch (18 cm) circle.

Tie the wire together, and add a ribbon loop as a hanger. Very carefully dot hot glue along the wire, fold the lace over, and hold until dry, doubling it for a fluffy effect. Hot-glue mountain mint leaves around the inside of the lace circle, and then hot-glue on a selection of herbs and flowers: sweet Annie for fragrance, crested celosia, globe amaranth, strawflowers, and pearly everlasting.

Designer: **Alyce Nadeau**

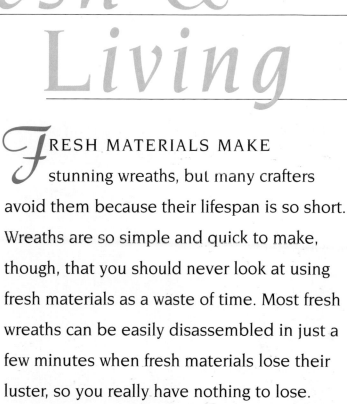

Fresh & Living

$\mathcal{F}$RESH MATERIALS MAKE stunning wreaths, but many crafters avoid them because their lifespan is so short. Wreaths are so simple and quick to make, though, that you should never look at using fresh materials as a waste of time. Most fresh wreaths can be easily disassembled in just a few minutes when fresh materials lose their luster, so you really have nothing to lose.

When working with fresh-cut flowers, you can prolong the life of the blooms with a few simple tricks. First, cut the stems at an angle and place them in clean water, removing any foliage that's below the water level. Next, condition the blooms by adding a preservative to the water and place them in the refrigerator for six to eight hours. Fresh flowers can be inserted into a base in water-filled floral tubes or attached to floral picks and inserted into wet floral foam. Finally, lengthen the lifespan of the blooms in your finished wreath by spraying them with a light coat of preservative spray to prevent them from losing moisture through their petals.

Spring Fling

THIS WREATH OF FRESH SPRING FLOWERS was creatively designed for lasting beauty.

To make the wreath, hot-glue flowers and foliage that will dry well in place directly to a vine base. The flowers in this wreath included acacia, sea foam statice, genista, and galax leaves.

Next, flowers needing special care to dry—roses, tulips, and stars of Bethlehem—were inserted into water-filled floral tubes. The tubes were then hot-glued to the base. Dried wood mushrooms and wild mosses were added around the tubes for variety.

As time passes, replace the flowers in the tubes with fresh flowers. The other flowers will dry in place and become a permanent part of the wreath.

Designer:
Cynthia Gillooly

Snapdragon Surprise

*Y*OUNG AND OLD ALIKE DELIGHT IN THE fanciful nature of snapdragons, from their ruffled skirts to their obliging habit of popping their mouths. The assortment in this wreath represents a full garden of color.

To make the wreath, cut individual stems to vary-

ing lengths and insert them into a thoroughly damp-ened oasis base, completely covering the wreath with blossoms. Arrange the colors to suit your taste, reserv-ing the brightest ones for prominent highlights. For an extra embellishment, loop a narrow satin ribbon among the blooms, securing the ribbon at several locations with floral picks.

Designer: **Nora Blose**

Garden Fresh

LUSCIOUS FRUIT MINGLED with fresh flowers makes a wreath guaranteed to set the mood for fine dinner entertaining. To create a similar wreath, remove most of the stems from several red rose blooms, a deep purple iris, and magenta carnations. Insert the stems into a well-soaked oasis base. (If you use the type that has a plastic backing, your table will be protected from dampness.) Fill in the sides with clusters of red grapes, some berried eucalyptus, and a few branches of variegated pittosporum. Add clusters of fresh grapes and lime sections with floral pins. Weave a length of glitzy ribbon around the wreath, securing it as needed with floral pins. Finish by hot-gluing small stems of annual statice, nerine lilies, and spring asters.

Designer: **Cynthia Gillooly**

Forest Fragrance

Neon-yellow lemons contrast nicely with dark magnolia leaves. To make this wreath, first attach magnolia leaves around the front of a straw wreath base with floral pins, making sure the leaves point outward. Then fill in the front of the wreath with short stems of fresh pine, attaching them with pins.

Next, attach clusters of boxwood to floral picks and insert them between the magnolia leaves. Now for the lemons. Pierce each one end-to-end with a piece of heavy (18-gauge) wire, leaving several inches protruding from each end. Fold the wire ends straight back, and push them through the base, front to back, tucking the ends into the back of the base. Hot-glue heads of red yarrow onto the greenery, and add a few cone flowers.

Designer: **Julianne Bronder**

Hens and Chicks

*H*OUSELEEKS, MORE AFFECTIONATELY known as "hens and chicks," are one of the most satisfying plants you can use for a living wreath. These members of the sedum family grow almost before your eyes, and each "hen" produces so many "chicks" that you may be tempted to make several wreaths to hold them all! To make the wreath, build a base from chicken wire, shaping it into a circle, square, heart, or whatever shape you desire. Line the base with sphagnum moss and fill the form with potting soil. Plant the sedums well apart to give them room to grow and multiply. Press each plant firmly into the soil, and cover the soil with pieces of sheet moss. Finally, spiral a fine-gauge wire all around the wreath to hold everything in place, making sure not to wire across the plants.

Designer: **Diane Weaver**

Cornucopia

*W*HAT COULD BE MORE festive than a wreath that celebrates the fruits of the harvest? To make this wreath, hot-glue the larger, heavier items—such as the gourds—to a grapevine wreath base. Attach the grapes to the base with floral pins, and attach the potatoes with toothpicks and hot glue. Last, hot-glue the red peppers and small clumps of moss into place.

Designer: **Cynthia Gillooly**

Living Wreath

*W*REATH BASES CAN BE CRAFTED INTO GARDENS for many living plants. Some garden shops and mail-order houses carry these types of bases pre-made, but you can make your own at home with not too much effort. To make the base you will need fine chicken wire, a heavy-duty stapler, moss, potting soil, wire cutters, plywood, and several cooperative plants.

First, trace the circle shape of a large straw or vine wreath base onto a piece of plywood and cut out the doughnut center and the outer edges. Then mold the chicken wire over the top of the wood base and staple it to the back side. Soak the moss in water and then pack it with equal amounts of potting soil into the chicken wire. Last, plant an assortment of succulents (or other suitable plants) around the wreath. To increase visual appeal, small mushrooms and fungi can be hot-glued to the moss.

Designer: **Cynthia Gillooly**

Note: Keep the wreath sitting flat for a few weeks so the plants can take root. The wreath can be hung indoors, although you may want to take it down when you water it every few days.

Long-Lasting Table Wreath

SUPPORTED BY A WELL-SOAKED RING OF WET FOAM, the materials in this fresh table wreath will last throughout the Christmas season. To make the wreath, insert stems of evergreens directly into the foam. Attach stems of English ivy to floral picks and insert them into the base. Attach the tangerines to the base by piercing them from side to side with a piece of heavy floral wire, leaving about two inches on each side. Bend the wire ends straight back and insert them into the foam. Hot-glue cinnamon sticks to the ends of picks and insert into the foam.

Designer:

Julianne Bronder

The Real Thing

*S*OME CARNATIONS ARE ARTIFICIALLY "enhanced" to give them a brighter color, but these vivid blooms are completely natural. With the flower heads tucked up tightly against one another, the effect is that of an unbroken coral ring.

To make the wreath, thoroughly soak an oasis ring base and cut the stems to about 1 inch (2.5 cm). Insert the blossoms so that the petals touch each other for a lush look.

Finally, place bits of boxwood and misty blue or caspia around the inner and outer edges.

Designer: **Janet Frye**

Bountiful Harvest

ALL THE COLORS, SHAPES, AND TEXTURES of autumn are tastefully combined with the bounty of a fruitful harvest in this big and bold composition. To make the wreath, start by stuffing a large, hollow grapevine base with fresh fruit (use artificials to reduce the weight if desired). Next, wire a few ears of Indian corn at the top and hot-glue pampas grass and pyracantha berries around the base. Complete the design by hot-gluing a few stalks of dried wheat around the wreath.

Designer:

Aubrey Gibson

Fresh Fruit Fiesta

A BOUNTIFUL FRUIT WREATH ENLIVENS your entry or front door, and cool weather will keep it fresh for weeks. It does make a heavy display, though, and requires a stiff wire hanger and a solid nail.

To make the wreath, first fasten a pineapple in the center of a straw base that has been covered with clusters of boxwood. Attach the pineapple to the base by using a wood dowel or piece of thin bamboo as you would a floral pick. Hide the ends of the dowel or bamboo by pushing them into the wreath form, and secure them in place with wire. Then make a wire noose around the leafy crown of the pineapple and lash the loose end of the wire around the top of the wreath. To fill in the sides, wire and hot-glue an assortment of fresh fruit, nuts, and berries to the base. Finish by creating small clusters of cranberries on wire stems and adding them to the wreath on floral picks.

Designer: **Clara Curtis**

Herb Garden Wreath

*A*LTHOUGH THE BLOOMS AND FOLIAGE IN this stunning herb wreath were added fresh, they will air-dry in place without much color or fragrance loss. To make the wreath, arrange stems of herbs in small clusters and attach them to a straw wreath base with floral pins. The materials in this wreath included bay, yarrow, feverfew, anise hyssop, baby's breath, oregano, roses, sage, crested celosia, horehound, tansy, and violets.

Designer: **Alyce Nadeau**

Rose Nest

ROSES ARE BY FAR THE MOST POPULAR flowering shrub throughout the world. They have been grown by every ancient civilization from China to the Mediterranean. The untamed look of this wreath made of bear grass provides an interesting counterpoint to these refined "Sonya" roses.

To construct this unusual base, divide the bear grass (or any suitable long grass) into three or four bunches, securing the bottom of each bunch with wire, string, or rubber bands. Loop the grass into a wreath shape, adding one bunch at a time, and gluing or wiring the bunches together. Be sure to leave some ends trailing freely. For a less vibrant color, the wreath can be set aside for several days in a hot, dry area, where it will fade to a pale, dusty green. To attach the flowers, wire a well-soaked oasis holder onto the base. Then arrange the roses in a loose triangle with the larger blooms nearer the foam and the smaller ones at the points of the triangle. Tuck bits of moss and extra rose foliage around the roses to camouflage the stems and holder.

Designer: **Janet Frye**

Bunches of Bouquets

*M*ANY FRESH FLOWERS ARE IGNORED BY wreath makers because they don't dry well. This dramatic wreath made from fresh azaleas may change your mind. F ror a multi-colored array, select several different types of azalea for your wreath. Cut some flowers from each, and cluster them together into small bouquets. Wire the bouquets onto floral picks and insert them into a moist oasis ring base. Create the abundance of color you see here by placing the flower clusters close together and covering every available angle of the oasis base.

Designer: **Nora Blose**

Perfect Pansy Wreath

*P*ANSIES ARE AMONG THE FIRST ANNUAL
plants to be set out in the garden because they
can easily withstand a night's frost. Ranging in color
from pure white to a deep, dark purple that looks
almost black, pansies are versatile, easy-to-grow plants
that fit into any landscape, and they make a wonderful
choice for a lush fresh-flower wreath.

To make this wreath, begin with a well-moistened
oasis base. Cut a basketful of pansies, and cluster
them into small bunches. To make it easier to insert
the delicate stems into the oasis, fasten each bouquet
to a floral pick. Then insert the picked clusters all
around the wreath base, packing the flowers together
for complete coverage.

Designer: **Nora Blose**

Radicchio and Grape Wreath

HERE'S AN EYE-CATCHING WREATH MADE FROM SIMPLE, everyday materials—fresh radicchio lettuce and grapes—that makes a great centerpiece for a buffet table. To make the wreath, first cover a small straw base with radicchio leaves, securing them on the back side with floral pins. Arrange grape bunches around the wreath and secure in several places with floral pins, then tuck a few sprigs of moss around the wreath for a natural look.

Designer:
Cynthia Gillooly

Autumnal Hues

𝓕RESH GRAPES ADD A NATURAL ENERGY TO this wreath, and they can be easily removed and replaced as needed. To make the wreath, hot-glue stems and sprigs of fresh eucalyptus, acacia, safflower, wood mushrooms, moss, and pin cushion proteas to a vine wreath base. Add small stems of fresh grapes with floral pins. The fresh materials will air-dry in place in a few weeks.

Designer: **Cynthia Gillooly**

Good Luck Wreath

*H*EATHERS ARE LOW-GROWING SHRUBS that can be found blanketing the ground throughout the British Isles where they are native. Heathers and their close relatives, heaths, are often planted in a mixture of varieties to obtain a tapestry of color and texture.

In folklore, heather brings good fortune and health. A family that has heather growing will have happiness. Representing two extremes of climate, the combination of fresh heather with eucalyptus may seem an unlikely marriage. The results in a wreath, however, are both gorgeous and fragrant.

To make this wreath, just combine small bunches of eucalyptus with three or four stems of heather and tie them to a birch base with yarn, using fine tweezers to thread the yarn between and around the branches of the base.

Designer: **Alyce Nadeau**

Breath-Taking Basil

*T*HIS FRESH WREATH COMBINES GREEN AND opal basil for contrasting foliage and flowers. This is a table wreath—the perfect centerpiece for, say, an Italian dinner. After it's too limp to admire, the leaves will still have plenty of flavor for a future spaghetti sauce. To make the wreath, start by saturating an oasis base with water. Insert sprigs of fresh basil into the wet foam. If the wreath is kept moist, it will remain fresh-looking for several days. It will also be fairly heavy.

Designer: **Alyce Nadeau**

Leprechaun's Gold

*O*T WAS THE VERDANT HILLS OF THE Emerald Isle, the leprechaun, and his pots of gold that inspired this lush green tribute to the patron saint of Ireland. To create this floral masterpiece first squeeze a straw base into an oval shape. Next secure about a hundred galax leaves (stems removed) in an overlapping pattern around the entire base. Wire a small round wet-foam floral block to the lower left side of the base and insert Oregon fern, seracena lilies (swamp lily or pitcher plant), Connecticut king lilies (or other yellow flowers), and fresh baby blue eucalyptus into the foam. Secure the pots of gold candy coins to the base and foam with floral pins.

Designer:
Janet Frye

Carnation Combinations

A STRIKING COMBINATION RESULTS WHEN you mix white carnations with shades of rose and deep, emerald green.

To make the wreath, start by inserting small stems of leatherleaf fern, lycopodium, and lemonleaf all around a well-soaked oasis base, making sure to alternate the greens to highlight the textural variety. Using the carnation blossoms as pinpoints of color, add about four dozen, again mixing the varieties so that each color is not concentrated in a single area. If you want the leaves to glisten as they do here, spray your wreath with a commercial preservative or with a home-made recipe.

Designer: **Beth Stickle**

Rhododendron in Bloom

THE MAGNIFICENCE OF THESE RHODODENDRON ENABLE AS few as a half-dozen stems to make a stunning wreath. To make this wreath, cut each stem with a sharp, angular cut, leaving enough of the stem so that the flower isn't flattened but shows its entire fullness. Then insert each one into a well-soaked oasis base.

Designer:
Beth Stickle

Airy Azalea Array

$\mathcal{F}$OR A MULTI-COLORED ARRAY, SELECT SEVERAL DIFFERENT TYPES of azaleas for your wreath. Cut some flowers from each, and cluster them together into small bouquets. To make handling easier, wire the bouquets onto floral picks before inserting them into a moist oasis ring. Create the abundance of color you see here by placing the flower clusters close together and covering every available angle of the oasis base.

Designer:
Beth Stickle

Bright and Bewitching

*T*HIS WREATH MAKES A STUNNING conversation piece for spring and summer dinner parties. To make the wreath, first hot-glue several large mushrooms around a grapevine wreath base. Hot-glue fresh-cut galax leaves over the mushrooms, and fresh flowers around the galax leaves. (Note: The flowers will stay fresher longer if you insert their stems into water-filled floral tubes.) To finish, hot-glue stems of dried globe amaranth, roses, white statice, lilies, and small clumps of moss between the fresh arrangements.

Designer: **Cynthia Gillooly**

Wonderful Silks

*T*HANK GOODNESS—SILKS have finally lost their stigma. Gone are the days when silk flowers were synonymous with fake flowers. Many of today's silks are so well crafted that even flower experts don't always immediately recognize them as faux. Working with silks offers many advantages to wreath designers. It's usually easy to find your favorite flower in many stages of bloom and in many colors, and you can rearrange them to suit your wreath simply by bending their wire stems. Foliage, berries, fruits, and vegetables are also available as silks, providing wreath designers with lightweight, versatile materials that have virtually endless design possibilities. Working with quality silks can get expensive, so don't be afraid to mix them with dried flowers from your garden, or cones and seed pods from your last walk in the woods.

Artichoke Wreath

MUTED BROWNS AND GOLDS SUGGEST autumn as an ideal time to make and display this dramatic Victorian wreath, made more interesting and unusual by the use of dried artichokes. These eye-catching design elements are easy to prepare: You can buy them at your local supermarket and hang them by their stems to dry.

To make this wreath, start by hot gluing dried caspia and silk fantasia cone flowers to an oval grapevine base. Next, weave a length of peach lace through the composition. Finish by wiring on the artichokes and a few pinecones.

Designers:
Aubrey Gibson,
Alecia Godfrey,
and Beth Welch

Spice Island

A BOUNTY OF FRUITS AND SCENTED SPICES bathed in the warm earth tones of autumn make this a classic harvest wreath. To make the wreath, start by pinning a ribbon of colored twist paper onto the sides of a straw base, creating loops that puff out at 2-inch (5 cm) intervals. Next, coat an assortment of plastic fruit with craft glue and roll them in a mixture of fragrant powdered herbs. (The designer for this wreath used a spice mixture of turmeric, oregano, parsley flakes, mustard, chili pepper, cinnamon, cloves, and marjoram.) Finally, hot-glue a large bow at the top of the wreath and small bouquets of baby's breath an cinnamon sticks around the wreath.

Designer: **Nora Blose**

Pastel Passion

$\mathcal{F}$LEXIBLE ARTIFICIAL TWIG BRANCHES WIRED to a heavy-gauge wire ring created the base for this wreath of pastel paper flowers. To make the wreath, first cut the silk twig branches into 8-inch (20 cm) lengths. Hold them against the base in small clusters and attach with floral wire. After you've covered the entire base, add interesting curves to the branches by gently bending them. Next, hot-glue the larger flowers into the branches, then add the lighter ones. Hot-glue stems of silk pussy willow and silk berries around the wreath. Finish by hot-gluing small white ribbon loops round the wreath.

Designer: **Fred Gaylor**

Della Robbia

A REINFORCED FOAM RING SERVES AS A sturdy base for this magnificent della robbia wreath. To make the wreath, first outline the base with with silk magnolia and boxwood leaves by inserting their stems directly into the foam. Next, wire a large tapestry-print bow to the top of the wreath. Arrange and hot-glue the silk flowers and fruits around the wreath next, beginning with the larger, heavier items.

Unlike most of the wreaths in this book, the materials in this wreath should be attached in two different directions: Start at each side of the bow and work your way down from both sides until you meet yourself in the middle.

Designer: **Fred Gaylor**

Peachy Keen

FLOWERS NORMALLY MAKE US THINK of spring and summer, but the use of silk flowers in soft, warm tones gives this wreath a decidedly autumnal flavor. To make the wreath, hot-glue clusters of silk lipidium and silk flowers to the base, then hot-glue an assortment of nuts, cones, and silk fruits around the wreath.

Designer:
Julianne Bronder

Thisaway, Thataway

THIS COLORFUL WREATH HAS STRIKING vertical and horizontal lines. To make it, form bunches of Sweet Annie and secure the stems with rubber bands or floral tape. (This wreath has eight bunches.) Attach the bunches to a straw base and secure with floral pins or with wire wrapped around the base. Wrap the wreath loosely with narrow ribbon, securing the ends with hot glue.

Place three tall cinnamon sticks, upright on the wreath and hot-glue them in place. Lay several dried yarrow stems (minus the heads) horizontally and hot-glue them in position. Hot-glue silk pansies onto the wreath. Choose several yarrow heads (the ones shown were dyed orange and rust with fabric dye), work them around the base of the pansies, and hot-glue them in place. Finish by hot-gluing a few pieces of yarrow vertically and small clusters of yarrow flowers along the horizontal stems.

Designer:

Janet Frye

Burgundy Blessings

A TRADITIONAL CHRISTMAS EVERGREEN WREATH TAKES
on a stunning new look in this wreath packed chock full of bur-
gundy-colored holly leaves. To make the wreath, start by attaching a bow
to a grapevine base with hot glue. Next, hot-glue small branches of silk
holly into the base. Last, add silk berries, plums, and lipidium until you
have a lush, full wreath.

Designer:
Julianne Bronder

Cherish the Past

IF THERE'S A SPECIAL CHILD IN YOUR LIFE, you've undoubtedly looked at those accumulations of toys and wondered how to keep the memories from slipping away. Or maybe you're a grandparent who long ago packed those memories into boxes and put them in the back of a closet or in a dusty attic. In this wreath, once-cherished alphabet blocks make a great design base for a child's wreath. To make the wreath, start by hot-gluing alphabet blocks (or other bright, lightweight toys) into a silk evergreen base. Next, cut a piece of foam to fit inside the bottom of the wreath and hot-glue it in place. Create an arrangement in the foam with stems of silk evergreens, then hot-glue more toys in place. Finish by hot-gluing small bouquets of baby's breath around the wreath and adding a cotton print bow.

Designer: **A Christmas House**

Roses and Ribbons

GREENS AND REDS ARE CERTAINLY THE most commonly used Christmas colors, but that doesn't mean you have to restrict yourself to traditional holly berries and pine boughs to capture the holiday spirit.

To make this wreath, start by wrapping a straw base with green velvet ribbon, leaving about 3 inches (7.5 cm) of the base uncovered at the bottom. Insert the stems of a dozen or so silk roses and a few sprays of artificial greenery into the straw to cover the exposed straw area. Fasten a ruffle of red velvet ribbon around the front surface of the wreath, securing with pearl-head pins. Finish by hot-gluing a silk rose blossom under every other ribbon loop.

Designers: **Aubrey Gibson,
Alecia Godfrey,
and Beth Welch**

Easter Bonnet Wreath

*T*HE EARLIEST WREATHS PROBABLY originated as headwear that later found a home on a wall or door. Here's a lovely Easter bonnet wreath that likewise serves both purposes. To make the wreath, hot-glue pink and blue tulle around the hat base, tying it in a large bow with streamers at the bottom. Next, hot-glue silk blooms and foliage to the netting. Finish by weaving several colors of satin ribbon around the flowers and into the tulle bow.

Designers: **Aubrey Gibson,
Alecia Godfrey, and
Beth Welch**

Beloved

*B*URSTING WITH RED AND PINK FLORAL splendor, this creation makes a welcome alternative to the traditional Mother's Day bouquet, and it will last much longer.

To make the wreath, hot-glue large silk blooms around the base, then weave and hot-glue stems of silk ivy around the base. Next, attach clusters of dried roses, globe amaranth, and caspia to floral picks and hot-glue them into the base. Fill in any bare spots with moss.

Designer: **Julianne Bronder**

Heaven Sent

*H*ERE'S A STUNNING EXAMPLE OF HOW successful a design can be that positions delicate flowers and a luminous ribbon on a large and sturdy grapevine wreath.

To make the wreath, first hot-glue stems of blue silk caspia around the vine base. Then glue on silk morning glories, small latex tulips, silk grasses, and blue silk flowers, with a full bouquet arrangement as the focal point at the bottom. Don't put any flowers on the top third of the wreath. Glue on the flocked latex ivy. Fashion a full bow with long streamers from moiré ribbon, and wire it to the top of the wreath, allowing the streamers to drape down.

Designer: **Cynthia Gillooly**

Welcoming Wreath

A RATTAN WREATH BASE AND AN assortment of silk flowers and greenery combine to create a colorful front door wreath.

To make the wreath, first hot-glue a 2-inch (5 cm) square block of floral foam to the inner rim of the base. Cover the foam with sheet moss using hot glue or floral pins. Create the floral arrangement next by picking silk flowers and greenery into the foam. To increase the drama of the design, hot-glue a large silk poppy at the top of the base.

Designers:
**Michael Staley
and Aubrey Gibson**

Ornate Oval Wreath

AN OVAL GRAPEVINE BASE HELPS CREATE the tableau setting of this wreath.

To make the wreath, start by wiring a large bow to the bottom center of the wreath. Cut stems of silk evergreens to varying lengths and insert them into the vine with a bit of hot glue on their stems under the bow. Finish the bottom arrangement by hot-gluing stems of baby's breath and silk berries into the bow and in the evergreens. To make the top arrangement, hot-glue a small cluster of evergreens to the top and hot-glue a bird in the center of the greenery. Hot-glue small stems of silk berries and baby's breath into the evergreens.

Designer: Julianne Bronder

Unity

*W*REATHS ARE WELL KNOWN FOR THEIR round and oval shapes, which were probably originally chosen for their symbolic meaning of fullness, completeness, and coming together. To make this wreath, first mark the center top of the wreath. Hot-glue stems of silk berries and blooms on both sides with their stems facing the center mark. Hot-glue a large bow with long streamers over the center mark, then weave the streamers down and through the vine.

Designer: **Cynthia Gillooly**

Impostor

*T*HIS STRIKING WREATH has a hidden secret: the designer deliberately purchased inexpensive artificial flowers from a discount store to demonstrate that beauty doesn't have to break the bank. To make the wreath, cut out two 3-inch (7.5 cm) blocks of floral foam and glue them to the top and bottom of the base. Create bouquets for the top and bottom of the wreath by hot-gluing stems of silk daffodils, African violets, roses, ivy, pansies, liatris, assorted pink and yellow flowers, and ivy into the foam. Pick the flowers and foliage into the floral foam. Finish by covering any bare foam with sprigs of moss.

Designer: **Luck McElreath**

For Mother, With Love

*H*ERE'S AN ELEGANT MOTHER'S DAY greeting delivered though the language of flowers. In Victorian times the rose was used as an expression of love, the color white signified purity, and the circle represented undying affection. To make the wreath, first hot-glue silk roses and foliage around a straw base. Next, form a large satin ribbon bow and pin it to the top of the base. Wind the bow's streamers down and around the wreath and tie them into a smaller bow at the bottom. Hot-glue two rose buds into the bow, then finish by hot-gluing sprigs of baby's breath around the wreath.

Designer: **Nicole Victoria**

Less is More

ⓄNE OF THE MOST IMPORTANT DESIGN skills is knowing when to do nothing. The maker of this harvest wreath recognized the simple grace of this swirling grapevine base and added just the right amount of soft color, shape, and texture to enhance its form without overpowering its natural beauty. To make the wreath, first hot-glue sprays of artemisia to the bottom of the base. Next, hot-glue della robia fruit to the artemisia and add a paper ribbon bow.

Designer: **Jeannette Hafner**

Something to Smile About

*E*NJOY A GARDEN OF SPRING BLOOMS THROUGHOUT THE winter with this spectacular floral wreath. To make the wreath, arrange and hot-glue paper (or silk) floral blooms around a moss base, taking care to face the flowers at a variety of angles. Finish by hot-gluing small sprigs of silk baby's breath into the gaps.

Designer:

Nancy McCauley

For Him

$\mathcal{G}$AME BIRD FEATHERS AND A PAIR OF well-used pipes distinguish this masculine Father's Day wreath as a handsome year-round decoration for any wood-paneled office or sportsman's den. To make the wreath, begin by wiring sprays of fragrant eucalyptus onto an oval grapevine base in a radiating background pattern. Next, hot-glue small sprays of German statice, gold wind branches, and berries onto the base. To create the focal points, hot-glue three large silk magnolias to the top of the wreath and hot-glue guinea and duck feathers around them. Finish by hot-gluing pipes and bird nest to the bottom of the wreath.

Designers:

Nora Blose and Michelle West

Positively Poinsettia

A LARGE SILK POINSETTIA BLOOM SETS the stage for this understated holiday wreath. To make the wreath, hot-glue stems of silk foliage, ever-greens, and seed pods around the sides of a grapevine wreath base. Hot-glue several stems of cedar down the center, then hot-glue a raffia ribbon and streamers over the cedar. Wire the poinsettia in the center and hot-glue small clumps of moss around the wreath.

Designer: **Cynthia Gillooly**

Victorian Age

*T*HIS VICTORIAN FLORAL WREATH USES A grapevine base as part of the design. To make the wreath, start by wiring a cluster of twisted bamboo across a grapevine base. Next, hot-glue stems of silk evergreens to the top and bottom of the bamboo. Finish by hot-gluing large and small silk flowers and silk berries to the greenery.

Designer: **Julianne Bronder**

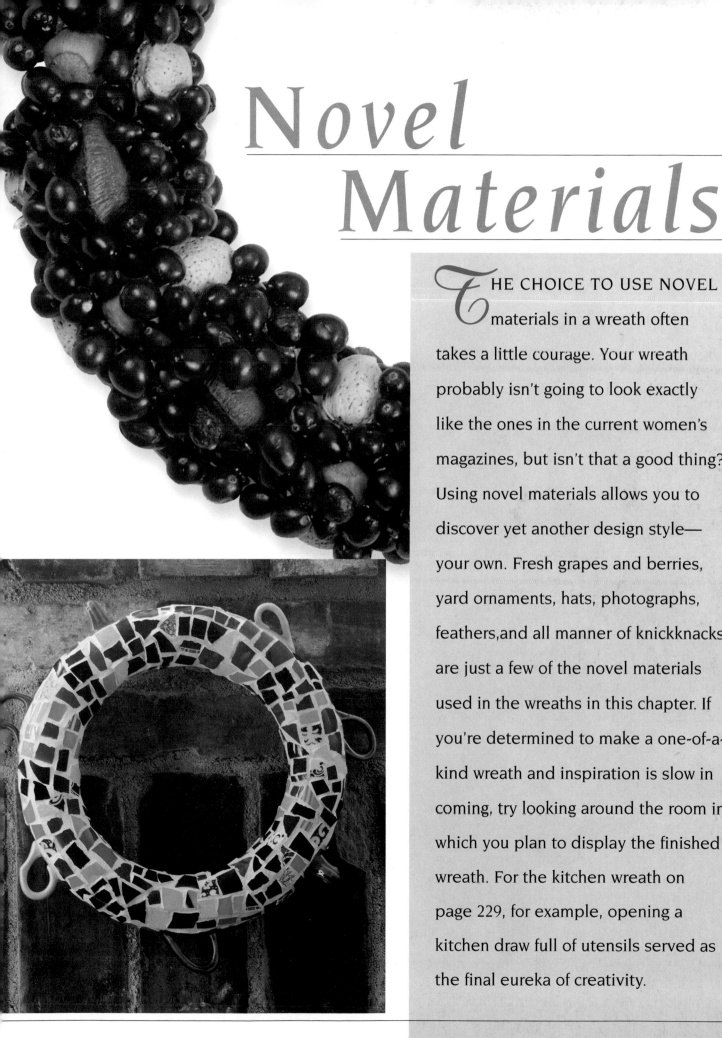

Novel Materials

T HE CHOICE TO USE NOVEL materials in a wreath often takes a little courage. Your wreath probably isn't going to look exactly like the ones in the current women's magazines, but isn't that a good thing? Using novel materials allows you to discover yet another design style— your own. Fresh grapes and berries, yard ornaments, hats, photographs, feathers,and all manner of knickknacks are just a few of the novel materials used in the wreaths in this chapter. If you're determined to make a one-of-a-kind wreath and inspiration is slow in coming, try looking around the room in which you plan to display the finished wreath. For the kitchen wreath on page 229, for example, opening a kitchen draw full of utensils served as the final eureka of creativity.

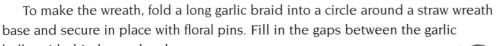

Garlic-Lover's Wreath

$\mathcal{S}$OME OF THE FINEST CUISINES IN THE WORLD WOULD BE NOTHING
without garlic, and one could argue the same about an herbal wreath.

To make the wreath, fold a long garlic braid into a circle around a straw wreath
base and secure in place with floral pins. Fill in the gaps between the garlic
bulbs with dried sage, bay leaves,
cinnamon sticks, star anise,
and red hot peppers.

Designer:
Sylvia Tippitt

Culinary Art

A COLLECTION OF KITCHEN UTENSILS, cinnamon sticks, and artificial berries form an interesting montage. To make the wreath, start by wrapping a foam base in ribbon, securing as needed with a glue gun. Next, hot-glue an assortment of kitchen utensils around the base, reinforcing with wire if needed. To keep the wreath low-cost, look for utensils in second-hand stores or clean out a few kitchen drawers.

Designer: **Cynthia Gillooly**

Make A Mosaic

A FOAM WREATH BASE MAKES A great canvas for a mosaic. To make this wreath, start by cutting ceramic plates in half with tile nippers. Continue breaking the plates into smaller and smaller pieces until you have pieces that are about ½ inch (13 mm). Be sure to wear safety glasses while you work.

Next, break six ceramic cups in half by gripping the edge of the cup's rim with the tip of the tile nippers and carefully squeezing the handles together. Carefully nip away at the half with the handle on it until the handle is attached to a small rectangular or oblong shard.

Decide where you would like to place the handles around the wreath, then butter the back of each handle piece with tile adhesive and attach it to the base. Repeat with the rest of the handles and let them dry for at least eight hours.

Cover the front of the wreath with the small pieces, buttering their backs with adhesive and positioning them about ⅛ inch (3 mm) apart. Trim the pieces with tile nippers to fit as needed. Cover as much of the inner and outer sides of the base as possible and let dry overnight. Turn the wreath over and cover the back side as you did the front. Let dry overnight.

Mix a batch of tile grout to the consistency of cake frosting, following the manufacturer's instructions. Wearing gloves, use a piece of polyethylene foam to spread grout over the surface of the wreath. Press the grout into the small spaces between the pieces until the surface of the wreath—front, back, and sides—is well covered. Allow the grout to set for 15 minutes, then use clean pieces of foam to wipe the surface clean, removing all excess grout on or between the ceramic pieces and on the cup handles. Let the grouted mosaic set for 30 minutes, then use a damp cloth or sponge to remove all traces of excess grout. Let the mosaic wreath dry overnight before hanging.

Designer: **Terry Taylor**

Just for Fun

*P*INK FLAMINGOS SET the tone for this fun wreath made from plastic lawn ornaments, silk flowers, and a ribbon-wrapped base.

To make the wreath, first wrap a foam base with ribbon, securing as needed on the back side with floral pins or sewing pins. Next, wire plastic flamingos to the base. Fill the area around the bottom of the wreath with a spray of silk blooms and foliage, feathers, glass baubles, and seed pods that have been sprayed with blue-green paint.

Designer: **Fred Gaylor**

Color Me Copper

VINE BASES CAN BE SPRAYED IN ANY COLOR paint to create colorful, seasonal bases.

To make this wreath, spray a vine base, grape leaves, and stems of eucalyptus with copper paint. Next, create the arrangement at the bottom of the base by attaching the materials to floral picks and hot-gluing the picks into the base. Next, add stems of wheat, dried sable, and dried roses as accents.

Designer:
Cynthia Gillooly

Nature Scene

CINNAMON STICKS PROVIDE AN ATTRACTIVE perch in this imaginative table wreath that brings a touch of nature indoors. To make the wreath, hot-glue two cinnamon sticks vertically to a grapevine base. Tie a third cinnamon stick across the others with wire, raffia, or string and then secure with hot glue. Cover the joints with small sprigs of moss. Next, hot-glue miniature lotus pods, artificial apples, cane twigs, mushrooms, evergreens, moss, and finally the birds to the base.

Designer: **Janet Frye**

'Tis the Season

*F*RESH CRANBERRIES AND BOWLS OF MIXED nuts are so popular at Christmas time that we immediately associate them with the holiday season. Used in a wreath, they send a cheerful Yuletide greeting that's bright in color and rich in texture. To make this wreath, start by hot-gluing mixed nuts evenly around the top, the inner, and the outer edges of a small foam base. Fill in the spaces between the nuts with cranberries. Note: To save time, wrap the foam base with red ribbon so you won't need as many berries to cover the gaps.

Designer: **Dawn Cusick**

Here Comes Peter Cottontail

*A*WHITE WREATH ON A DARK DOOR—WHAT could be more striking? This bunnytail wreath would impress even the bunnies. To make it, you'll need white and red bunnytails, both available at craft shops. Wire the white bunnytails into full bunches, about 4 inches (10 cm) wide and 6 inches (15 cm) long. Then wire the bunches to a grapevine or wire wreath base, overlapping them so that the stems are covered. For a full, lush look, make sure to cover the inside and outside diameters, as well as the front. Next, wire together small bunches of red bunnytails, attach to picks, and insert them into the wreath at random.

Paint some tiny baskets gold (these are 1 inch wide and 2 inches high, or 2.5 by 5 cm). Wire a pick to the back of each basket, and hot-glue a sprig of greenery inside, at the back. Glue dried roses, celosia, and globe amaranth inside each basket, to make miniature arrangements. Pick in the baskets around the wreath.

Form a bow from gold wired-net ribbon and wire it to the wreath, arranging the streamers around the wreath and wiring them into position.

Designer: **Diane Weaver**

Angelic Glory

CERAMIC ANGELS FLOAT IN A BACKGROUND of silver-king and silver-queen artemisia in this pastel holiday wreath. To make the wreath, form small bunches of artemisia and secure the stems with rubber bands. Attach the bunches to a foam or straw wreath base with floral pins. Trim the final bunches as needed to create a nice overall shape. Next, hot-glue lamb's ear, strawflowers, and the angels into the artemesia background. Make a bow of narrow satin ribbon, drape the streamers across the center of the wreath, and glue the ends in place.

Designer: **Janet Frye**

Woodland Angel Wreath

ATURAL MATERIALS SELECTED IN COLORS to complement a parchment Christmas angel create a Yuletide wreath that's a feast for the eyes. To make the wreath, wire the paper angel onto a large oval grapevine base. Next, bind a sheaf of wheat with wire and spray it with copper paint, then wire it to the base. Work a length of French ribbon around the grapevine and a touch of Christmas greenery with hot glue. Hot-glue eucalyptus, lotus pods, and parchment roses, canella berries, and gold twigs around the wreath. Finish by adding small clumps of moss and blue beading.

Designer: **Cynthia Gillooly**

Nursery Wreath

*S*WEET AND RADIANT DESCRIBE THIS NURSERY wreath, perfect words to describe the new baby, too. To make the wreath, start with a white-washed grapevine wreath. Make a bow with long streamers from cotton tapestry ribbon, drape the streamers around the wreath, and use glue to secure them to the base. Next, glue dried caspia around the bow. Tie on the shoes. Give the baby a kiss.

Designers:

Cynthia Gillooly and Jamie McCabe

Welcome to the Family

THIS SIMPLE AND DELICATE WREATH ARTFULLY combines blue and pink, making it perfect for a baby boy or a baby girl. To make the wreath, cut blue satin material in 2-inch (5 cm) strips with pinking shears and wrap them around a foam base, using dressmaker pins to secure. Wrap lace ribbon over the satin. Fashion a lace bow with long streamers, and wire the bow onto the wreath. Pin the streamers to the lower part of the wreath. From the pink cord, make a bow with long streamers and pin it onto the lace bow. Pin the ends of the streamers to the wreath. Glue on silk foliage and pink lilac flowers. For a final lacy touch, glue on the fern.

Designer: **Julianne Bronder**

Easy Eucalyptus Wreath

ONG ADMIRED FOR ITS FRAGRANCE, eucalyptus also makes a versatile wreath background. For the wreath shown here, cut long branches of eucalyptus into 4-inch (10 cm) pieces and then wire them individually to a wire ring base. Next, hot-glue cinnamon sticks, walnuts, almonds, dried caspia, and pyracantha berries into the eucalyptus.

Designer: **Corinne Erb**

'Shrooms

A SWEET HUCK WREATH BASE AND LARGE dried mushrooms form a naturally contrasting background for delicate dried flowers. To make the wrath, hot-glue thin stirps of sheet moss around the top surface of the wreath. Position and hot-glue the mushrooms around the moss, then hot-glue small groupings of roses, ambrosia, poppy pods, zinneas, queen-anne's-lace, butterfly bush, veronica, princess feather, and delphinium in the spaces between the mushrooms.

Designer: **Joan Naylor**

Memories

TREASURED MEMENTOS ADD SPECIAL SIGNIFICANCE TO YOUR HOLIDAY creations as in this very personal Mother's Day wreath. To make the wreath, first cover a straw base with white paper ribbon, then wrap over the paper ribbon with a glitzy, iridescent ribbon and pink tulle. Finish by attaching a hat, gloves, pearls, family photos, and a tussy mussy.

Designer:
Michelle West

Gift-Giving Wreath

A SELECTION OF FRAGRANT GIFTS IS featured in this thoughtful Mother's Day wreath. The items can be removed from their decorative boxes, leaving the wreath intact for display in mom's bathroom or bedroom. Start with a purchased silk greenery wreath and tie the gift boxes and sachets on with peach cording. To finish, weave a length of white lace randomly through the greenery and hot glue on several pink silk roses.

Designer: **Nicole Victoria**

All Aflutter

GREAT SELECTIONS OF FEATHERS CAN BE bought in bulk from most craft stores. To make this wreath, insert the feathers directly by their stems into a foam base, taking care to insert them all at the same angle. To make the bow, fold lengths of copper ribbon in half together and attach them to floral picks. Insert the picks into the base to create a bow shape, then pick in several clusters of unfolded ribbon.

Designer: **Dawn Wade**

Spectacular Spuds

SMALL RED POTATOES AND MOSS MAKE A QUICK, SIMPLE WREATH. Just attach the potatoes into a foam base with wood picks, hot-gluing for reinforcement. Finish by filling the gaps with small clumps of moss. Eventually the potatoes will spoil, but that only gives you an excuse to make a new wreath!

Designer:
Cynthia Gillooly

Masquerade

CREATE AN INSTANT PARTY WITH THIS festive New Year's or Mardi Gras wreath. To make the wreath, first form a base from braided electric wire that has been sprayed with copper paint. Attach a hat at the top of the wreath with wire and top with ribbon. Attach sprigs of silk flowers, ribbon, and a party shoe to the bottom of the base.

Designers:
Michael Staley
and Aubrey Gibson

Caroler's Wreath

*W*EAVE A MUSICAL THEME THROUGH YOUR next holiday wreath and attract bands of roving Christmas carolers to your door. To make the wreath, wrap a foam base with a length of silk evergreen garland, securing as needed with floral pins. Next, wire a small faux violin in place and weave gold ribbon around the wreath. Add a large bow to one side of the wreath. Spray several magnolia leaves and baby's breath blooms with gold paint and allow them to completely dry, then hot-glue them to the wreath. Finish by hot-gluing a red silk bloom, an angel ornament, yarrow blooms, and sumac blooms around the wreath.

Designers:

Nora Blose and Michelle West

Green Thumb Wreath

A COLLECTION OF CLAY POTS, A HANDFUL of bulbs, and a few hand tools make a decorative statement for the home gardener.

To make the wreath, first attach the tools to a wire-reinforced base with a length of heavy-gauge wire and reinforce with hot glue. Next, hot-glue clay pots all around the wreath: about a dozen and a half clay pots in two different small sizes, facing them in different directions and adding the smaller ones last. Glue several tulip bulbs into some of the pots and at other likely locations.

Pin loose grapevine to the outside of the wreath to frame the composition and hot-glue short stems of silk blooms into the vine. Finish by filling in any open spaces with Spanish moss.

Designer: **Julianne Bronder**

Hot Stuff

ESSENTIAL TO SOUTHWESTERN CUISINE, large red ancho peppers make an arresting Christmas wreath in any part of the country.

To make this wreath, wrap a wire-ring base with raffia to create a wide, flat surface for attaching materials. Hot-glue on the peppers first, then follow with accents of miniature corn, eucalyptus sprigs, cone flowers, nuts, and pods. A wired raffia bow adds a final splash of color.

Designer: **Janet Frye**

Feathered Friends

CLUSTERS OF SMALL BIRD NESTS (purchased at a craft store) add a special touch to this magnificent wreath. To make the wreath, start by covering a straw wreath base with moss that you can collect from the forest floor or purchase in sheets from a floral supplier. Insert alder twigs, complete with their seed pods, into the base so they radiate from the outer edge. Next, attach small branches and individual leaves of magnolia, galax, and Virginia pinecones to floral picks and add them to the wreath. To finish out the natural look, wire crab apples and pears in place.

Designer: **Clara Curtis**

Lassoed Laurel

*H*ERE'S PROOF: LITERALLY ANYTHING CAN be used as a wreath base! This wreath, built upon a hank of rope, was inspired by a late-night western movie. To make it, loop a piece of rope several times, and wire it together at the top around four 6-inch (15 cm) wooden picks. (The picks will provide stability and a firm base for fastening the decorative elements.) On the front side, hot-glue several stems of silk Canadian pine, natural eucalyptus, and a few mahogany pods. Add dried pomegranates, a miniature lotus pod, and a few artificial pears and berries. For a bit of whimsy, hot-glue a mushroom bird (bits of lichen form its wings and tail) to the lowest loop of the rope.

Designer: **Janet Frye**

Glitter and Glisten

SO YOU WANT TO MAKE AN UNUSUAL wreath? Fashioned from hot glue and glitter, this one-of-a-kind wreath can be made as small or large as you like. Simply coat a piece of glass with cooking oil spray and squirt layers of hot glue in a circle, dropping glitter between each layer. Form a bow and ribbon streamers at the top. Once the glue cools, just peel it off the glass. For a colorful bow, paint the back surface of the bow with an acrylic paint.

Designers:

Aubrey Gibson and Michael Stayley

Soap on a Wreath

THIS CHARMING WREATH DOES double duty: The bayberry-scented soaps emit a soothing fragrance, while the wreath adds charm to the room it's displayed in. To make the wreath, wrap a wooden base with a narrow satin ribbon all the way around. Create sections of narrow lace ribbon on the surface of the wreath base and secure the ribbon in place by stapling or gluing it to the back side of the base. Last, hot-glue the soaps and the bow to the wreath base, then create a ribbon loop for hanging at the top.

Designer: **Julianne Bronder**

Index